PROPH

PROPHESY!

Tony Higton

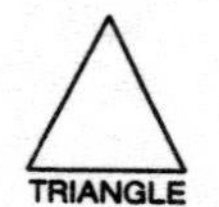

First published in Great Britain 1998
Triangle Books
Holy Trinity Church
Marylebone Road
London NW1 4DU

ACKNOWLEDGEMENTS

Bible quotations are from the
New International Version © 1973, 1978 and 1984

British Library Cataloguing-in-Publication Data

A catalogue record of this book is available from the British Library

ISBN 0-281-05106-2

The views expressed by the author are not necessarily those of the publisher.

Typeset by Pioneer Associates Ltd, Perthshire
Printed in Great Britain by
Caledonian International, Glasgow

This book is dedicated to my wife and partner in prophecy, Patricia, and to all those who have prayed for my public ministry, many of whom I have never met.

CONTENTS

ACKNOWLEDGEMENTS

I want to express my thanks to my wife, Patricia, for checking the manuscript and giving me the benefit of her theological, prophetic and literary skills; to our administrator Guy Harper and computer boffin Geoff Estall for sorting out an esoteric computer problem and to Peter and Moira Brown for the loan of their house in Norfolk as a writing retreat. I also want to thank the members of Hawkwell Church for their consistent prayer and support for this project.

Tony Higton

1 *A PROPHETIC CALL*

'I think you should remember that your salary is paid by the Church of England.' I felt somewhat put in my place by these words from a middle-aged church member. She and her husband were committed Christian people from the polite, respectful, pro-establishment Anglican stable. I had publicly criticized the church and she had felt this wasn't cricket.

It all began two years after I was ordained. Having joined the Church of England in 1964 by conviction, after being brought up in an independent church, I was more pro-Anglican than most. It was helpful to me, as a newcomer with an evangelical background, to discover that the bishop who was to ordain me in 1967 stood in that same evangelical tradition. Imagine my devastation when the newspapers reported in 1969 that he was having an adulterous affair with an actress.

At the same time, as a young curate looking after the parish in an interregnum, I found myself caught up in a determined political move by the diocese to weld together three disparate churches in an early team ministry experiment. The protests of the congregations fell on deaf ears, but it was twenty years before the thriving church where I had begun my ministry recovered fully from the negative effects of that episode.

During the early 1970s, before we moved to Hawkwell, I found myself conveying news items to prayer gatherings that indicated all was not well with the Church of England and with our society. Somehow it seemed effective: folk really prayed in depth. But in those days this was an occasional emphasis.

Gradually, this aspect of the ministry developed during the early years in Hawkwell, while we were majoring on the renewal of the parish's life, worship, prayer and evangelism. God gave us numerical growth and a strong sense of being a united, outward-looking community. The church was gripped by a vision of mission which led them to send my wife, Patricia, and me to many parts of the world encouraging and resourcing local churches to be united for every-member intercession, ministry and evangelism. A canon theologian commented recently that in many ways we were prophetic in those positive aspects of church development – ahead of our time as God gave us insights as a couple about how to implement every-member ministry and mission. The result is that for ten years 90 per cent of our church members have been actively involved in the work of the church, for which we praise God.

But the profound concern about the problems in the Church of England would not go away. Through the charismatic movement we mixed with a whole range of Christians – from Catholics to housechurch people. Seeing it in such a broad context highlighted the weaknesses of the Anglican Church. Sometimes the grass certainly seemed greener on the other side. And yet I loved the richness of the liturgy of the Church of England and the dignity of its ceremonial. I valued its historical continuity and wealth of tradition. And I believed the comprehensiveness of the parish system and the potential influence for good upon the nation to be great assets.

At various crucial points in our pilgrimage God seems to have led us to offer back to him the things which are precious to us: the ministry we were involved in; the place where we lived. For example in 1983 we came to a point where we were prepared to serve God in Israel, but we were prevented at the 'eleventh hour'. A similar thing happened in February 1984 over our position in the Church of England. For a few months we had seriously been considering leaving the denomination because of what we saw as serious failings.

We couldn't continue to live in limbo. We had thought and prayed a lot about it – a decision must be made. What mattered was not our feelings about the church or about leaving it, but rather knowing what God was saying to us. I therefore arranged a short private retreat from the parish.

So on a cold February afternoon I drove twenty miles into the Essex countryside to a fairly deserted conference centre.

Later in the day, in private prayer I offered up to God my ministry and security in the Church of England as well as any desires to leave it. This was no pious ritual. I've learnt over the years that if you offer things to God in this way he has a habit of taking you up on it!

I had no idea how God would speak to me or what he would say. All I knew was that he had brought me to a point of being genuinely ready to do his will. My daily reading was from Lamentations – not a book that suggests itself as a source of guidance in such circumstances.

As I read about a situation far more devastating than anything which had happened to the Church of England, I sensed the danger of dire consequences if the church did not repent. Nevertheless I felt I glimpsed something of the heart of God towards the church. The mixture of deep sadness and love expressed by the prophet was surely inspired by the Holy Spirit: 'My eyes fail from weeping, I am in torment within' (2.11).

The writer's analysis of the causes of Judah's downfall seemed relevant to the situation in the Church of England: 'The visions of your prophets were false and worthless; they did not expose your sin' (2.14).

His message was one of hope and challenge:

> Yet this I call to mind and therefore I have hope: Because of the Lord's great love we are not consumed, for his compassions never fail. . . . Though he brings grief, he will show compassion, so great is his unfailing love. . . . Let us examine our ways and test them, and let us return to the Lord. Let us lift up our hearts and our hands to God in heaven, and say: 'We have sinned and rebelled'. . . . Restore us to yourself, O Lord, that we may return; renew our days as of old.[1]

The thought that struck me most was that God had not abandoned his failing people. But the prophet was called to share God's grief over his beloved nation. With this thought came the overwhelming sense of call. I was not to pull out of the Church of England – I was to stay put but not to stay quiet. Although I have never been tempted with any delusion of grandeur to compare myself remotely with the biblical prophets, yet I was to follow the example of the writer of Lamentations – to share God's grief over the failings of the church and to call God's people to repentance.

However much I may fail in fulfilling this call from God, I do not think I could live with refusing to obey him. But saying 'yes' to such a calling is like signing a blank cheque for God. I suppose that's one definition of faith. I had no idea what I was letting myself in for. I was to find much of it very difficult and unpalatable, and some of it nerve-wracking! Had I known in February 1984 all that it would mean I probably would have been tempted to follow Jonah's example to emigrate!

As it was, within a couple of months, David Jenkins, the Bishop-elect of Durham, had publicly denied the virgin birth and cast doubts on the bodily resurrection of Christ. When there was a resounding silence from the evangelical wing of the church, I knew this was the time to go public. Resulting from this Action for Biblical Witness to Our Nation (ABWON) was born.

The Church of England understands the roles of pastor and teacher quite well, although it mistakes some inspiring, provocative teachers for prophets. There may be prophetic elements to their ministry but they are not prophets in the biblical sense. The church also has some (in my view, limited) understanding of the apostolic role of bishops. In recent years, as the emphasis has begun to swing towards mission, it has begun to understand the role of evangelist too. But it finds great difficulty coping with the prophetic role unless prophecy takes the form of a call for social justice (which is, of course, a vital aspect of prophecy). It does not help that prophetic people (including myself) are imperfect and get things wrong. But that is also true of apostles, evangelists, pastors and teachers.

All institutions have a powerful tendency towards self-preservation. Consequently they find criticism and calls for change threatening. The Church of England is a largely conservative institution and so is particularly prone to feel threatened. Yet criticism and calls for change are essential aspects of prophetic ministry. The church can easily see prophets as mere irritants, apparently arrogantly and judgementally threatening the status quo.

But the prophetic ministry is vital to the welfare of the church, as Scripture and, for that matter, common sense indicate. An organization which is not self-critical or does not carefully weigh up criticism or resists calls for change, will fossilize and die.

Both the Old and New Testaments teach the importance of prophecy. It is to be eagerly desired as a gift (1 Cor. 14.1, 39). Prophetic understanding may come in the dramatic form of visions and dreams (Num. 12.6; Acts 2.17), supernatural knowledge (2 Kings 6.12; John 4.19) or sudden revelation of God's purposes. More often it comes through listening to the 'gentle whisper' of the Spirit of God (1 Kings 19.12), based upon studying the word of God in the Scriptures. The prophet will measure the situation he or she is facing (whether in the local or wider church, or the nation) according to the plumb-line of God's word, then speak forth God's 'now' word into the situation.[2]

The gift is given by God to encourage, strengthen and comfort his people (1 Cor. 14.3); to remind them of his will and faithfulness and to confront compromise over fundamental doctrine, immorality or injustice. At times the prophet is called to rebuke sinners and to warn of judgement.[3] He or she may also make predictions, but this is only one element of prophecy.[4]

God has appointed prophets (amongst other ministries) in the church (1 Cor. 12.28; Eph. 4.11). In fact the church is built on the foundation of the apostles and New Testament prophets such as Zechariah, Anna, John, Jesus, Philip's daughters, Agabus, Judas, Silas and various others.[5]

Part of the divine strategy seems to be summed up in Amos 3.7–8: 'Surely the Sovereign Lord does nothing without revealing his plan to his servants the prophets. The lion has roared – who will not fear? The Sovereign Lord has spoken – who can but prophesy?' This passage also clearly describes the prophetic obligation to speak which I described above: 'The Sovereign Lord has spoken – who can but prophesy?' Sadly many Christian leaders seem to have not a prophetic obligation to speak, but a pathetic determination to keep quiet!

Christians are urged not to treat prophecy with contempt (1 Thess. 5.20). In fact a duty to respect but weigh prophecy is laid upon the people of God (1 Cor. 14.29). The prophet must be biblically orthodox, particularly concerning the person of Christ (1 John 4.1–3), and must be seen to show the fruit of the Spirit resulting from a relationship with Christ (Matt. 7.15–23).

I find it ironic that there are conservative Christians who fervently claim to be biblically orthodox, but nevertheless believe charismatic gifts and ministries such as prophecy are no longer available to the church. They think that New Testament passages urging us to seek them are no longer relevant today. According to such folk, these gifts have been replaced by the New Testament canon. I fail to see any distinction between such an argument and the arguments, which these conservatives would roundly reject, that other parts of the New Testament are no longer relevant to us.

There is no biblical justification for teaching that the gifts have ceased already. In fact the New Testament teaches when they will cease, namely, 'when perfection comes' and 'the imperfect disappears'; 'when we shall see face to face'; 'when I shall know fully' (1 Cor. 13.10–12). This is clearly referring to the consummation of all things, when the Lord returns. Some equate prophecy with preaching. I do not deny that some preaching may be prophetic. But the New Testament makes a clear distinction between prophets and teachers in the church (Acts 13.1). Having said all this, I want to stress that all prophecy is subject to Scripture and must be tested by Scripture. If it conflicts with Scripture it must be rejected.

The church needs prophets, alongside all the other gifted ministries. But to be prophetic is a costly ministry. In the next chapter we examine some aspects of this cost.

2 *OUTGROWING THE NICE GUY SYNDROME*

'Mr Tony Higton, Bigots Incorporated' read the address on the envelope. It did not take all my prophetic insight to discern that the letter inside was less than positive! It was anonymous except for a scrawled, indecipherable signature and the postmark was 'Mount Pleasant' – the only pleasant thing about it. The message, typed in capitals, was:

> What a poor and sad creature you are when you can find nothing better to do than straight away jump on the anti-gay bandwagon and have yet another go at something you simply do not understand.
>
> You display all the usual signs of a wretched, uncaring person who claims to be a Christian. Christ never once condemned homosexuality – he clearly had more sense than people like you.
>
> You will suffer your sad state of mind for a long time – closet homosexuals always do suffer and it is so sad.

I include that letter because it is the most recent I have received, arriving just a fortnight before I wrote this chapter. It is nowhere near the worst of the many hundreds of vitriolic, often anonymous, letters sent to me. Some of them are blasphemous. I have some sympathy with the writer of the letter quoted. He or she may be a homosexual or a close relative or friend of a homosexual. There is a heart cry amidst the aggression which inspired my prayers for the person concerned.

All I had done, however, was to write to *The Times* correcting a false impression given by the General Synod Press Office that the Church of England accepts 'committed, faithful' lay homosexual relationships. I pointed out that actually the official line was reaffirmed by General Synod in an amendment to my 1987 private member's motion, namely that homosexual practice 'was to be met by a call to repentance'.

How do you cope with the widespread unpopularity which a public prophetic ministry can engender? The first thing to do is to seek to be sure of your ground biblically. This means not only ensuring your message is theologically accurate but also checking the way it is put over. It is not easy, even after over twelve years of receiving such letters, to know someone thinks you are 'a poor and sad creature' who is 'anti-gay' and 'a wretched, uncaring person who claims to be a Christian'. The time when I find it easy will be the time to give up. And the time when I no longer examine my motives, words and actions, even after the most vitriolic and grossly inaccurate letters, will be the beginning of the end.

The Example of Christ

It is important to go back to the example of Christ. The western world's image of Christ is largely based on folk memories of songs like 'Gentle Jesus meek and mild'. As a study of historical theology clearly shows, the church takes on board much of the cultural baggage of the surrounding society.

Obviously the real Jesus did exemplify gentleness and humility. After all, it was he who said: 'Come to me, all you who are weary and burdened, and I will give you rest. Take my yoke upon you and learn from me, for I am gentle and humble in heart, and you will find rest for your souls' (Matt. 11.28–29).

When the disciples turned away the children whose mothers were bringing them for blessing, Jesus rebuked them and took the children in his arms to bless them. He had compassion on the crowds 'because they were harassed and helpless, like sheep without a shepherd' (Matt. 9.36). In his compassion he healed the sick.

He wept at the graveside of Lazarus and over an unbelieving

Jerusalem. Although he told her not to sin again, he refused to condemn the woman caught in the act of adultery. In humility he washed his disciples' feet. And he prayed for those who crucified him with the words: 'Father, forgive them, for they do not know what they are doing' (Luke 23.34).

So Jesus epitomizes humility, meekness, gentleness and compassion. Thank God that he does, because he is the supreme revelation of the Godhead. Without such qualities in the divine character we would be lost and hopeless. And since we are called to be Christ-like we too must show humility, meekness, gentleness and compassion. All of this is the acceptable face of Christianity according to western culture.

But that is not the whole story! I fail to see how anyone can read the Gospels and conclude that Jesus is *only* humble, meek, gentle and compassionate.

In various ways, Jesus made himself thoroughly unpopular. Because of his 'hard teaching' (John 6.60), challenging people to a discipleship based upon 'feeding on him' as the bread of life, '*many* of his disciples turned back and no longer followed him'. He thought even the Twelve might leave, too (John 6.66–67). In fact he had warned that his teaching would result in division, even within the family (Luke 12.51–53).

On several occasions he firmly rebuked the fear and lack of faith of the disciples, for example, when they were afraid in the violent storm on the lake (Matt. 8.26; 14.31), or when they were unsuccessful in exorcism (Matt. 17.14–21). He even gently rebuked the grieving disciples on the road to Emmaus for their unbelief about his death and resurrection (Luke 24.25–26).

When Peter, in misguided human compassion, tried to dissuade Jesus from going to the cross, Jesus said to him: 'Get behind me, Satan! You are a stumbling-block to me; you do not have in mind the things of God, but the things of men' (Matt. 16.23). Peter would hardly have enjoyed such a strong rebuke.

There are only two explicit references by Jesus to 'the church' recorded for us in the Gospels. One is his statement that he would build his church (Matt. 16.18). The other is his teaching on reconciliation. He teaches that an erring brother is to be approached privately by the person he has offended. If this is unsuccessful in bringing about repentance and reconciliation, that individual is then to take two or three witnesses with him. If that fails, the church is to be informed. And should that fail, the offender is to be treated as out of fellowship (Matt. 18.15–17). To gauge how popular this teaching is, it is only necessary to seek to put it into practice in the modern church!

Jesus not only rebuked and corrected his disciples. He also strongly rebuked those Pharisees who hypocritically rejected him. He publicly called them a 'brood of vipers' who were 'evil' and therefore could not do anything good (Matt. 12.34). He called them 'hypocrites', 'sons of hell', 'blind guides', 'blind fools', 'whitewashed tombs'. He said, 'You snakes! You brood of vipers! How will you escape being condemned to hell?' (Matt. 22.18; 23.13–17, 19, 23–33). He was angry at their hardness of heart (Mark 3.1–6).

On another occasion he said they were liars, children of the father of lies (John 8.44, 47, 55). When his disciples told him he had offended these Pharisees he responded by saying that they should be left alone as blind guides (Matt. 15.12–14).

Jesus cleansed the temple by driving out with a whip all the sheep and cattle on sale, scattering the coins of the money-changers and overturning their tables. How embarrassing to the devotees of a Jesus who is solely 'Gentle Jesus, meek and mild'!

His teaching on the end times would go over like a lead balloon in some polite Anglican circles! In his great prophecy of the signs of the second coming and the end of the age in Matthew 24, twenty-four of the thirty-one verses (77 per cent) refer to 'doom and gloom'. The end times will include war, famine, earthquakes, pestilences and revolutions. Twelve out of the fourteen specific references to 'hell' as a place of punishment in the New Testament are from the lips of Jesus.[1]

It is crystal clear from the Gospels that Jesus is not only humble, meek, gentle and compassionate. He is also the prophet whose hard teaching lost him many disciples and caused division, even within the family. He firmly rebuked the lack of faith of his disciples; taught church discipline for the persistently impenitent; strongly rebuked hypocritical religious leaders; used physical force to cleanse the temple and sometimes taught a sombre message of judgement and hell. Little wonder he was unpopular in various quarters!

Jesus makes it very clear that if he, the Master, was unpopular, ignored and persecuted, we should expect to be so too (John 15.18–20). He added elsewhere: 'It is enough for the student to be like his teacher, and the servant like his master. If the head of the house has been called Beelzebub [the prince of demons], how much more the members of his household!' (Matt. 10.25).

However we live in a culture which is dominated by the feel-good factor, by individualism and consumerism (alias selfish materialism). It is the supermarket syndrome. 'If I do not like that brand there are twelve others next to it . . . I will pick and choose to suit myself.' The pressure is on us to take that approach to Christianity – to choose the nice bits and ignore (or, at least, soft-pedal) the unpleasant aspects, like following Christ in risking unpopularity or persecution.

The Desire for Acceptability

One of the pitfalls therefore in the modern church (particularly a state church) is of Christians hoping to be acceptable to society and compromising in order to maintain that acceptability; or, in Jesus' words, of belonging to the world rather than living as those he has chosen out of it. We have forgotten the words of Jesus: 'Woe to you when all men speak well of you, for that is how their fathers treated the false prophets' (Luke 6.26). That verse should be mounted on the study wall of every Christian leader.

But it is not just in the world that modern Christians (including leaders) are tempted to compromise. Many seem to be afraid of the reaction of their congregation, their peers and of those over them.

We all have a need to be liked, a desire to be accepted. Only nutters look forward to being unpopular and hope to be persecuted. But to be prophetic means being willing to risk unpopularity or persecution. Little wonder few seem to accept a call to be prophetic, and those who do, constitute a serious threat to comfortable Christians.

There is great pressure to toe the line and only say what people want to hear. It is nothing new. The messengers from King Ahab said to the prophet Micaiah, 'Look, as one man the other prophets are predicting success for the king. Let your word agree with theirs, and speak favourably' (1 Kings 22.13). Isaiah condemns those who 'say to the seers, "See no more visions!" and to the prophets, "Give us no more visions of what is right! Tell us pleasant things, prophesy illusions. Leave this way, get off this path, and stop confronting us with the Holy One of Israel!"' (Isa. 30.10–11). Micah puts it picturesquely: 'If a liar and deceiver comes and says, "I will prophesy for you plenty of wine and beer," he would be just the prophet for this people!' (Mic. 2.11).

I understand such pressure only too well. Coming from a Free Church background and overcoming my suspicion of Anglican ways, I fell in love with the Church of England. Although 'Series 2' Communion had just been authorized, the worship was often from the Book of Common Prayer. I loved its depth and comprehensiveness, and the sheer beauty of its language. It opened up to me the riches of worship for the first time. The dignified but simple ceremonial of the services appealed to me, although I was still working through a tension between a profound appreciation of more complex ritual and symbolism on the one hand and a deep-rooted suspicion of anything not traditionally 'evangelical' on the other. I have a strong sense of history and the historicity of the Church of England had a powerful effect on me.

Given such reactions, it was easy to be caught up by the power of an institution like the church. And that is exactly what began to happen. It was partly a sense of the numinous[2] and partly a sense of being admitted into a humble but privileged place in the hierarchy of a church rich in historical splendour. I was ordained in Southwell Minster, one of the most beautiful Norman buildings in the country. I felt so honoured yet so insignificant against the background of the centuries as well as the pomp and ceremony. Similar thoughts occur to me whenever I am in York Minster for the Eucharist of the July General Synod each year. The archbishops, dressed in splendid robes, process solemnly down the aisle. Compared with us lesser mortals in mufti, they seem so dignified. But against the lofty arches of the Minster which soar heavenwards, they appear very insignificant.

The negative experiences of the Church of England I had during my first curacy in Newark were a shock, but did not destroy these early reactions. In 1970 we moved to Cheltenham to what is now a team ministry. In those days many of the people in the four churches were good people but ultra-conservative evangelical. You would not have found even a cross in the parish church and candles would have been anathema! The relationship with the diocese was distant, apparently by mutual agreement.

I could never be happy with such a situation and, where possible, sought to build bridges with the diocese. I got involved with the work of the Diocesan Youth Chaplain and I joined a clergy study group which met in the beautiful setting of the cathedral.

Difficult though some people might find it to believe now, in my early years after ordination I learned how to 'get on' in the church. That is why I am embarrassed when I come across ambitious clergy who are doing just that. I knew what to say and what not to say. I knew who to get involved with and how to be in the right place at the right time. I understood how to work the system. I still do, but I have a shrewd suspicion I have blotted my copybook in a big way! Had I continued to 'behave myself', who knows where I would have been now. (Not in the centre of God's will, that is for sure!)

The fact that I was also, in my early years in Cheltenham, often majoring on social and political issues (which I still regard as very important), could also have helped me to 'get on'.

In view of all this, I understand those ambitious clergy who work the system and cultivate popularity for their own advancement. I know how some of them attempt to justify their ecclesiastical climbing as altruistic ('I am doing it so I can have more influence for good in the church'). But I am profoundly saddened by it. When they stand before God, how much of their privileged ministries will be 'burnt up' as 'wood, hay or straw' (1 Cor. 3.10–15)? Although it is obviously right for some to receive promotion, that should be as a result of faithfulness, humility and entrusting their future to God.

Not all clergy (or lay leaders) are called to be prophets, of course. But we are all called to prophetic action at times, for example, expressing strong disagreement and criticism concerning the failings in the church when necessary. Such is not the way of improving career prospects.

In Old Testament days some of the false prophets 'prophesied' for personal gain. The Lord laments through Jeremiah: 'From the least to the greatest, all are greedy for gain; prophets and priests alike, all practise deceit. They dress the wound of my people as though it were not serious. "Peace, peace," they say, when there is no peace' (Jer. 6.13–14). Through Micah he condemns 'the prophets who lead my people astray, if one feeds them, they proclaim "peace"; if he does not, they prepare to wage war against him' (Mic. 3.5).

Some false prophets simply spoke their own opinions as if they were the word of God.[3] One used 'prophecy' to intimidate an opponent (Neh. 6.14). Jeremiah says some of his contemporary 'prophets' are 'but wind and the word is not in them' (5.13). The Lord sums up the desperate situation in Judah through him: 'A horrible and shocking thing has happened in the land: The prophets prophesy lies, the priests rule by their own authority, and my people love it this way. But what will you do in the end?' (5.30–31).

Ezekiel is called to prophesy against the prophets of Israel who speak out of their own imagination (13.2–3). Jesus warns against dishonest prophets: 'Watch out for false prophets. They come to you in sheep's clothing, but inwardly they are ferocious wolves' (Matt. 7.15).

If we are not going to give way to the strong temptation to seek acceptability we shall have to face up to the trauma of losing popularity.

The Pain of Rejection

God chooses the most unlikely people to fulfil his purposes. I would have thought I was in some ways the last person he would have chosen to speak prophetically in such a public fashion about the failings of the Church of England.

I was a sickly, nervous child who was, perhaps inevitably, overprotected by a loving mother. It did not help that, because of her illness, I had been separated from my mother for the first few weeks of my life. The main thing I remember about my early birthdays was being ill. I started school only to be rushed into isolation hospital for almost two months with scarlet fever followed by measles. As a very insecure child, being almost entirely separated from my parents for so long was traumatic. Shortly afterwards I remember being allowed to go late to school for a period of time because I was on medication for a nervous condition. Frequently, I was off school, enjoying the security of home. I was also very sensitive, often feeling deeply hurt as a result of incidents which another person might not have noticed.

My father was a committed Christian and occasional lay preacher. He was a man of prayer, who every morning at 5 a.m. would spend a long time with God, including praying for me. I may never know how much I owe to his prayers. But he was also a shy and fearful man. I too was painfully shy and picked up his fear. Like him I became a fearful, negative thinker. Because of all this school was a struggle, even though I did fairly well academically.

During my mid-teens I decided I was tired of being a wimp. I wanted to be one of the boys and so forced myself out of my shell and deliberately chose to be involved in some more risky activities. For example, I joined the school rugby team. I was totally useless at the game but that did not matter as much as it may seem, because the team was not much better!

So I broke out of my overprotected childhood, but at a high cost. I was still suffering inwardly from deep-seated fear and negative thinking. My philosophy seemed to be: 'If it can go wrong, it will go wrong and if it cannot go wrong it still might do anyway!' Although there was improvement these problems were not to be finally resolved until I received counselling and healing in 1981, just three years before the prophetic call came.

I shall return to the subject of fear later. But another aspect of my story is relevant here. Because of my insecurity and oversensitivity, I had a deep need for affirmation by other people. I needed to feel accepted. This was why I had broken out of my childhood caution as a teenager. I wanted to be one of the in-crowd, and I succeeded for the rest of my school career.

Even after the initial healing, I perhaps retained for a number of years a slightly above-average amount of sensitivity, fear and desire to be accepted. This was hardly conducive to a calling to confront the whole Church of England hierarchy, as well as the media and opposing pressure groups about the failings of the church. And yet, perhaps it was not entirely unhelpful. Doubtless it made me more self-critical and conscientious about a calling fraught with pitfalls.

But it also made coping with unpopularity particularly painful. For my first three years as Rector of Hawkwell I sought to be popular, but eventually I had to give in to the prompting of the Holy Spirit and address the persistent wrong behaviour manifested by a few influential lay leaders. I did so in private conversation as gently and lovingly as possible. But the reaction was negative and in one or two cases furious. I went through agonies and became very unpopular in certain quarters. But the conviction that, while avoiding legalism, we must practise what we preach kept me on course. I had to learn to off-load in prayer the threat and pain onto the Lord. This was important for the parish but it was also a preparation for the wider prophetic ministry which was yet to emerge.

When the Durham Controversy flared up in 1984 I wrote to all 11,000 clergy in the Church of England. Although precipitated by David Jenkins' denial of credal doctrine, the letter covered other serious doctrinal aberrations amongst clergy: compromise of the uniqueness of Jesus as the only Saviour in interfaith worship and the toleration, or even justification, of sexual immorality (heterosexual as well as homosexual) within the church.

The letter was basically a call for all grass-roots clergy to stand up and be counted over these fundamental issues. Being rather green in those days I do not think I gave two thoughts to the possibility of negative responses. I anticipated the wrath of some of the bishops, including the Bishop-designate of Durham. But I suppose I made two naive assumptions: one, that only positive clergy were likely to respond and the other, that the situation amongst the clergy was not as serious as I subsequently discovered it to be.

My education on these two points was soon underway. Out of some 2000 immediate replies (an amazing response to an unknown clergyman) about two-thirds were positive. But there were also 653 negative letters from clergy. Of these 370 were fair; 189 were rude, some vitriolic; 94 were anonymous; and some of them were quite sick. Remember I had only written to clergy.

In the early days, while these replies were arriving, I felt the need to get away to be alone with the Lord at frequent intervals. I remember walking through the fields near our home feeling emotionally bruised, battered and almost in a daze at the continuing onslaught. With that and disturbed nights, I was on a crash course in coping with unpopularity.

The following year I was amazed to be elected to General Synod. I anticipated this responsibility with a combination of expectation and dread. One of the main problems I had was not knowing where I stood with people. True, a good number of my fellow clergy in Chelmsford Diocese had voted for me (that accounted for the amazement!) But where did I stand with synod members or with the bishops? That question has stayed with me through most of my twelve years on the synod.

There are various problems in English Anglicanism which led to this uncertainty. Firstly, unlike the Americans, most English people are about as good at affirming one another as they are at speaking Norwegian. We may be embarrassed by the fulsome affirmation beloved of our American cousins, but that is preferable to the ambiguous politeness at which we excel.

Another problem is the forked-tongue syndrome. Many Christians will be polite, friendly and apparently completely positive, even though they may privately (or in conversation with others) think you are, for example, a fundamentalist cretin. Not that I am against being pleasant, even to antagonistic opponents. Because of my public image, I have frequently surprised people who have never previously met me by being warm and friendly. Actually that is my normal approach to life, even with my opponents within the church. The difference between this and the forked-tongue syndrome is that they know where I stand and what I think of their views or behaviour.

So one difficulty I have had, particularly in synod, has been relating to people who are friendly without my knowing what they really think of my views and actions. Obviously I cannot go round asking them what they think about me! And because I have been rocking the synodical boat, as well as speaking out controversially in the media, I have tended to feel faintly paranoid.

One aspect that could not be put down to my subjective feelings was the reaction to my speeches. It reached the point where, whenever I stood up to speak in a debate, I sensed strong negative vibes and even heard audible groans. Applause is almost mandatory after any speech in General Synod – even the most appalling drivel gets a hand. But in my case applause tended to be non-existent or apparently from a dozen enthusiastic friends around the chamber! Much of this was simply a reaction to what I believe to be a genuinely prophetic word to the synod. But I eventually learnt important lessons about where I was at fault, too – namely, I believe I delivered true words from the Lord, but couched in language which was in the style of the biblical prophets. I failed to realize that, had I used phraseology which was more culturally sensitive, without diluting the message, more people would have responded positively. I also did not balance my critical remarks with sufficient affirmation – but more of that later.

During the period from the late 1980s until 1995, I grew to hate going to General Synod. I still felt called to be a member; I enjoyed some of the fellowship and the most vital debates were interesting. But basically, I really hated being so unpopular. At the same time the prophetic obligation to confront the doctrinal and moral confusion in the church remained as strong as ever. So I never had the slightest intention of backing off from fulfilling that to the best of my ability, not only because it was a divine calling but also because of my concern for the Church of England and its mission to the nation.

I found the pilgrimage out of the nice guy syndrome very painful indeed. I was consoled by the fact that even the great biblical prophets experienced rejection. Stephen reproached his persecutors with the question: 'Was there ever a prophet your fathers did not persecute? They even killed those who predicted the coming of the Righteous One.'[4] Jesus, who himself as a prophet was rejected in Nazareth, laments over Jerusalem: 'O Jerusalem, Jerusalem, you who kill the prophets and stone those sent to you' (Matt. 23.37).

Jeremiah certainly suffered a great deal of rejection. He was ignored or attacked. The priests had him beaten and put in the temple stocks. The men of Anathoth threatened him, 'Do not prophesy in the name of the Lord or you will die by our hands' (Jer. 11.21). The priests and prophets also called for him to be executed.

Hosea criticizes the people of God because 'the prophet is considered a fool, the inspired man a maniac' (9.7–8). That has a remarkably modern ring about it. Call yourself a prophet in many circles today and people will put you on a level with a man who thinks he is a poached egg!

In view of the persistent rejection of his prophets there is little wonder the Lord announces: 'They made their hearts as hard as flint and would not listen to the law or to the words that the Lord Almighty had sent by his Spirit through the earlier prophets. So the Lord Almighty was very angry. "When I called, they did not listen; so when they called, I would not listen," says the Lord Almighty' (Zech. 7.12–13).

Jeremiah had to learn to depend on God and to transfer onto the Lord through prayer the pressure coming from his persecutors. He prayed: 'Listen to me, O Lord; hear what my accusers are saying!' (18.19). This is a very powerful form of prayer, but perhaps not one in common use today. Asking God to listen may seem illogical, in that God knows what will be said to us before we hear it. But then, from one angle, all petitionary prayer seems illogical since God knows what we need before we do. The benefits of a prayer like Jeremiah's include reminding ourselves God is with us in our difficulties and that, as the cross shows us, he bears our burdens. It also reminds us, as Paul discovered on the Damascus road, that to persecute Christians is to persecute Christ. So, in such a heart cry we become conscious of the Lord identifying with our pain. There is healing in this sort of prayer.

Jeremiah also knew that God has his ways of protecting persecuted prophets (as well as persecuted Christians in general). When King Jehoiakim sent men to arrest Jeremiah (and Baruch the scribe) we read the intriguing statement: 'But the Lord had hidden them' (Jer. 36.26). Obviously, biblical history shows that this does not mean prophets will never suffer. But even then God will be there for them. When King Zedekiah handed Jeremiah over to his officials because his prophecies were regarded as treasonable they put him, unbeknown to the king, in a water cistern where he sank in the mud and was likely to starve. But a Cushite official in the royal palace heard of his plight and told the king who had him rescued.

A more spectacular experience of God's protection of prophets took place almost 300 years earlier. Elisha's servant was terrified to find they were surrounded by a hostile Aramean army: '"Oh, my lord, what shall we do?" the servant asked. "Don't be afraid," the prophet answered. "Those who are with us are more than those who are with them." And Elisha prayed, "O Lord, open his eyes so he may see." Then the Lord opened the servant's eyes, and he looked and saw the hills full of horses and chariots of fire all around Elisha' (2 Kings 6.15–17). In other words the servant was granted a vision of the angelic protection around Elisha. Angelic protection is, of course, not just for prophets but for the people of God in general. But it is a particular help to Christians who are threatened or persecuted to know that it is there.

The corollary of this divine support and protection is that the prophet must persist in his ministry even if he is rejected and persecuted. So God said to Ezekiel:

> The people to whom I am sending you are obstinate and stubborn. Say to them, 'This is what the Sovereign Lord says.' And whether they listen or fail to listen – for they are a rebellious house – they will know that a prophet has been among them. And you, son of man, do not be afraid of them or their words. Do not be afraid, though briers and thorns are all around you and you live among scorpions. Do not be afraid of what they say or terrified by them, though they are a rebellious house. You must speak my words to them, whether they listen or fail to listen, for they are rebellious. (Ezek. 2.4–7)

In the light of this divine support, protection and strength, as well as his or her divine calling, the prophet can, when rejected or persecuted, face the challenge of Jesus' words to all who are persecuted: 'Blessed are those who are persecuted because of righteousness, for theirs is the kingdom of heaven. Blessed are you when people insult you, persecute you and falsely say all kinds of evil against you because of me. Rejoice and be glad, because great is your reward in heaven, for in the same way they persecuted the prophets who were before you' (Matt. 5.10–12).

So those called to prophetic ministry are to press on with that ministry as conscientiously as possible, following Jesus who was not merely a 'nice guy', facing up to and seeking to rejoice amidst the pain of rejection and even persecution.

3 *COMMUNICATING THE PROPHETIC WORD*

I remember many years ago an evangelical clergyman saying we should not make *public* criticism of David Jenkins' (very public) denial of aspects of credal doctrine. He is now a bishop! Yet public confrontation of public compromise over fundamental issues is part of a prophetic ministry.

Other aspects of this ministry, as we have seen, include encouraging, strengthening and comforting God's people; reminding them of his will and faithfulness; confronting immorality or injustice; sometimes rebuking sinners; and, on occasions, warning of judgement or predicting future events.

The encouraging, strengthening and comforting side is a great ministry but, in terms of personal cost, it is not difficult. People are not rejected for encouraging, strengthening and comforting. They may even be promoted! I shall return to this very important side of the ministry later.

The Courage to Criticize

The crunch comes with confronting compromise over fundamental doctrine or immorality, rebuking sinners and warning of judgement. Such concepts are alien to our easy-going society. (Confronting injustice is sometimes more acceptable, depending on the issue being addressed.)

In our western culture, dominated as it is by relativism and pluralism, to affirm absolute norms of truth or morality is widely unacceptable. Basically we make up our own truth or moral values as we go along. What matters is what is true for the individual. All the belief and value systems are thought, generally speaking, to be of equal validity. We all win and we all get prizes.

Affirmation of a particular system of basic beliefs and morality is acceptable, but claiming any such system is absolute, i.e. required of everyone, is now considered heretical. Worse, to assert that those undermining this system are wrong and, in the case of the church, should if they persist ultimately be disciplined, is an even greater 'heresy'. Yet these 'heresies' are fundamental to a prophetic ministry. Little wonder prophets are unpopular today.

It is illuminating that many bishops are willing to affirm the truth but not to drive away error. Yet Canon C18 of the Canon Law of the Church of England states that bishops are not only 'to teach and uphold sound and wholesome doctrine'. They are also obliged 'to banish and drive away all erroneous and strange opinions'.

However it is very rare to come across bishops doing the latter. As children of our age they are (to some extent unconsciously) heavily influenced by relativism and pluralism. And they have, more often than not, seriously failed the church by not publicly confronting the scandalous undermining of credal doctrine and basic morality in certain sections of the church. A number would make, for example, public speeches affirming the bodily resurrection of Christ, without overtly speaking against the undermining of that view. They appear not to understand that serious *public* offences require *public* correction for pastoral and evangelistic reasons. Yet such a public prophetic ministry is required of bishops both for the protection and encouragement of those harmed or distressed by the offences, and to dispel confusion in the minds of those not yet involved in the church. It cannot be achieved without both affirmation of truth and confrontation of error.

If the bishops keep quiet or only affirm the truth, the impression given is that it is acceptable within the church to hold their view *and* the heretical or immoral views scandalizing many of the faithful. The result is confusion. A number of bishops doubtless correct clergy – where necessary – privately, but if the offence of that clergyman is in the public domain, bishops owe it to congregations and the wider public to make a public correction.

They need to follow the example of the apostles who exercised a prophetic ministry in exposing and condemning the views of false teachers. Paul warned the Corinthians about false apostles in the church who rejected his apostolic authority. We may parallel them with modern Christian leaders who reject the authority of apostolic (biblical) teaching. Paul called them servants of Satan (2 Cor. 11.13–15).

He warned the Galatians of false teachers in the church who were undermining the gospel with 'another gospel' of salvation by works. He calls down a curse on them (Gal. 1.8–9). He warns other churches against false teachers and their deceitful scheming and hollow philosophy (Eph. 4.14; Col. 2.8).

John also calls false teachers in the church who deny the incarnation 'antichrists' (1 John 2.18f.) and he warns of false prophets (1 John 2.18f.; 4.1). Peter condemns false teachers who exploit the faithful (2 Pet. 2.3).

Paul was not only specific about failings and solutions, but named names. He named Demas, who had deserted him (2 Tim. 4.10). He also named Alexander and warned the believers about him, although he was, of course, an unbeliever (2 Tim. 4.14). Similarly the prophets publicly named people in their words from the Lord, not only to their face but also indirectly.[1]

Many of the bishops are good men who conscientiously perform their diocesan duties and fulfil a pastoral role in caring for clergy. Some of them have been working away behind the scenes, fighting for truth on committees, councils and within the House of Bishops. They have at times suffered unfair opposition, even vilification, because of their stand for the truth; and they are determined to continue in this witness. I accept all this and thank God for it.

Nevertheless they have failed the church very seriously in not giving a public prophetic witness over the scandalous controversies afflicting the church in recent years. When they are pressed to comment on them they seem to live up to the saying: 'The bishops of the Church of England are, generally speaking, generally speaking!'

Christianity claims to be the absolute truth. Biblical morality claims the status of absolute values. That is scandalous in our society. But there is little scope for prophetic ministry without this foundation of absolutes. The great controversy in the Old Testament was whether Yahweh was the only God,[2] or whether he could be worshipped alongside other gods. The prophets strongly affirmed the former. In the same way the New Testament affirms the uniqueness of Christ as the only Saviour.[3]

Similarly biblical morality (bearing in mind the importance of reading the Old Testament 'through' the New Testament) is absolute and will be part of the basis of final judgement. We are saved by grace but judged by works (Rev. 20.12–13; cf. Eph. 2.8–9).

We have seen that critical prophecy has always been unpopular because of the pride and selfishness of human beings. But because of the antagonism towards affirmations of absolute truth and values in our relativist and pluralistic society, it is doubly unpopular today. Add to this the modern sentimental definition of love as only being nice to people and this increases the unpopularity of prophecy. A prophetic ministry today therefore is increasingly difficult to fulfil.

I have said enough earlier to show that I am no stranger to fear. Before I received counselling and healing in 1981, not infrequently I experienced quite serious attacks of fear. Sometimes the fear was irrational: it had no known cause but was simply the combination of the insecurity and negative thinking which I described earlier. I managed to cover all this up (which did not help) with an English, clerical, male mask, but the problem was I was trapped in my own prison. The later years in Cheltenham and some of the early years in Hawkwell were characterized by this problem.

In those early Hawkwell years, while the fear remained, the Lord enabled me to make radical changes in the worship, not least introducing an almost totally spontaneous evening service which I found quite traumatic and emotionally draining to lead. He helped me to tackle some quite serious incidents which required firm church discipline and to face some traumas in the church which, at times, seemed to threaten its survival. The emotional cost of all this was enormous. Looking back I do not know how I survived, let alone came through successfully. And yet I do – it was a remarkable experience of the sovereign grace of God. I mention this not to claim any credit – there is none to claim – but simply to testify that God can enable us to continue in obedience even in the midst of such fear.

In Hawkwell, the result was that the Lord brought about in depth renewal to the whole church in the 1980s, together with extraordinary fruit in evangelism, widespread corporate intercession, and every-member ministry based upon a deep unity. At least 1000 churches in the UK and overseas have used the resources we have produced which witness to these principles.

The other fact I can testify to is that God can deliver us from deep-seated fear. I was counselled by an older minister and a very experienced woman counsellor. It was the first time I had opened up to anyone about the fear. When at length they came to pray for me (with my ready consent) a strange thing happened. I suddenly felt a deep resistance to their prayers. Yet I felt this was not my real attitude. It was as if I were a spectator, watching something happen to me. The clergyman sensed this and prayed authoritatively against it. After this they prayed for healing.

Some sixteen years later I can affirm that the results of that prayer were quite remarkable. The intense fear disappeared. As I said earlier, I perhaps retained for a number of years a slightly above-average amount of sensitivity and desire to be accepted. It lasted well into the time when God led me into the public prophetic ministry within the General Synod, the church and the media.

I remember walking past Church House, Westminster, shortly after I was first elected to General Synod but before my first synod. The prospect of standing up in front of all those people, some of them very able debaters, and confronting the whole House of Bishops (including my favourite northern bishop of the time!) filled me with dread. I decided I simply had to make a speech on my first day in the synod, otherwise I might remain silent for ever! I did speak – probably my briefest speech ever – but it was important for me because it broke the ice. Since then, threatening though it sometimes is to give a speech, I have not looked back.

A certain amount of fear is normal in life – some of it is beneficial. At times the audacity of some of our campaigns or the confrontational nature of some of my statements continued to engender a certain degree of anxiety about negative reactions or consequences. But one must press on regardless.

I have included a description of my own experience of fear for two reasons. One is that it may encourage those who wish to obey God in a prophetic ministry but are fearful. The other is that fear is the main reason why those who should speak out do not. I want to challenge such people to speak out anyway, and for them to know the challenge comes from someone who knows what fear is and has experienced God's grace overcoming it.

Micaiah was an example of a prophet who did not give way to fear in spite of pressure. King Ahab said to Jehoshaphat: 'he never prophesies anything good about me, but only bad' (1 Kings 22.18).

When the Lord called Jeremiah his response was: 'Ah, Sovereign Lord . . . I do not know how to speak; I am only a child.' But the Lord said to me, 'Do not say, "I am only a child." You must go to everyone I send you to and say whatever I command you. Do not be afraid of them, for I am with you and will rescue you' (Jer. 1.6–8).

The Lord continued that Jeremiah was to be primarily a prophet of doom to the nations and only secondarily a prophet of restoration. In the light of this very daunting task the Lord reassured him further: 'Get yourself ready! Stand up and say to them whatever I command you. Do not be terrified by them . . . They will fight against you but will not overcome you, for I am with you and will rescue you' (Jer. 1.17–19).

It is perhaps worth repeating at this point that I in no way compare myself with the prophets of the Bible, many of whom risked their lives as they confronted the kings and priests of their day. Jesus continued a divine ministry of encouragement to fearful prophets:

> What I tell you in the dark, speak in the daylight; what is whispered in your ear, proclaim from the roofs. Do not be afraid of those who kill the body but cannot kill the soul. Rather, be afraid of the One who can destroy both soul and body in hell. Are not two sparrows sold for a penny? Yet not one of them will fall to the ground apart from the will of your Father. And even the very hairs of your head are all numbered. So don't be afraid; you are worth more than many sparrows. Whoever acknowledges me before men, I will also acknowledge him before my Father in heaven. But whoever disowns me before men, I will disown him before my Father in heaven. . . . Whoever finds his life will lose it, and whoever loses his life for my sake will find it. (Matt. 10.27–33, 39)

There is no excuse for giving way to fear when God has called us to fulfil a particular ministry, in this case, prophetic ministry. Those who rely on the strengthening grace of God will overcome their fears and know his protection and deliverance. They can be encouraged by knowing that God loves them and knows everything about them and their needs. And Jesus the great High Priest acknowledges them before the Father in heaven.

Knowing all this and beginning to face up to the pain of outgrowing the nice guy syndrome with its desire for acceptability prepared me for the main campaigns we have launched within the Church of England.

The Ministry in Practice

I believe God called me primarily to speak prophetically to the Church of England, addressing its current doctrinal and moral failings. Speaking prophetically directly to society is a secondary aspect. Others will be called to major on that. It is very important to be clear as to one's particular calling, otherwise energy will be dissipated.

Back in 1984, just before I wrote to all the clergy in England, I gave much thought to the title of the organization we were setting up. My concern was to call the church back to its biblical basis, not as an end in itself but as a means to fulfilling its mission to the nation. Also I did not want a mere talk shop or moaning society, I wanted action. Having a gift of never using one word when several will do, it was not long before I reached 'Action for Biblical Witness to our Nation' (ABWON).

Credal doctrines

In 1985 we encouraged our supporters to write to their bishops asking for a public statement of their views on the three theological issues raised in the Durham Controversy: the virginal conception and bodily resurrection of Christ and the less-publicized issue as to whether a Christian had to believe Jesus was God in the flesh. We had an excellent response in terms of the number of replies. Nowadays bishops are wise to the fact that the media will seize on their responses and as a result are far less likely to reply to a questionnaire as Reform[4] has discovered.

However, the answers gave great cause for concern, revealing that, at the time, our bench of bishops did not excel in orthodoxy. The need for a prophetic witness became even more apparent. The replies were as follows:

Those who regard it is necessary believe that:	Diocesan	Suffragan	Both
Christ is 'God made flesh'	33%	41%	37%
The virgin birth was a historical event	61%	59%	60%
The resurrection of Christ was a bodily resurrection	67%	59%	63%
Those who would allow bishops to hold unorthodox views	45%	15%	32%
Those who replied but refused to answer the questions or were unclear	30%	33%	32%
Number of replies	33(57%)	27(44%)	60(57%)

Later that year I presented to Dr Runcie a petition signed by 20,000 Anglican communicants, asking for only orthodox bishops to be appointed in future. It was my first visit to Lambeth Palace and the archbishop received me graciously. He spent a whole hour listening to my concerns and said he would convey them to the Crown Appointments Commission.[5] At the end he leaned across, put his hand on my knee and prayed an extemporary prayer. I was impressed.

In the autumn of that year I was elected to General Synod. At the end of the first day I was standing chatting to a couple of friends in the vestibule of Church House, Westminster, when the archbishop came down the stairs. He made a bee-line for me, put his hand on my shoulder and said, 'I hope you are not too discouraged, Tony.'

I felt that he was seeking to win me over by being nice to me. After all, it is not everybody who has the Archbishop of Canterbury giving him an hour of his time in the splendour of Lambeth Palace and being so solicitous after his welfare.

It is easy to disagree strongly and publicly with someone from a distance. But my experience is that when you mix with 'liberals', syncretists, gay activists and the like you discover that often they are nice people. On experiencing this, many Christians find it very difficult to retain as strong a prophetic witness against these people's errors as they did from a distance. This is one of the main reasons why people who become involved in the church structures or the hierarchy all too frequently lose their cutting edge. (I would at this point add that theological liberalism is changing radically in the 1990s – the views which reached their low point as expressed by such writers as Don Cupitt and John Hick, are now regarded as discredited in academic circles. The Bible is taken much more seriously in those circles and dialogue between liberals and evangelicals is more productive. However, what happens in academia can take twenty years to filter through to the church.)

God forbid that we should harbour personal antagonism or convey uninformed and inaccurate criticism. But the 'niceness' wins these people over and they begin to compromise where they should not. How many prophets have been silenced in this way?

Later it seemed clear to me that Dr Runcie was irritated when he discovered he had failed to win me over. This annoying

Essex clergyman was not going to keep quiet. From then on I felt that his responses to my probing questions in synod were sharp and even cynical.

I continued through speeches, questions, articles and interviews to press for correction of the damage done by the Durham Controversy. In November 1986, after ABWON had mobilized thousands of Christians to pray, the Houses of Clergy and Laity, by a large majority, reaffirmed belief in the virgin birth and the empty tomb.

In July 1987 a major debate took place on the bishops' report *The Nature of Christian Belief*, which was a response to the Durham Controversy. The report acknowledged that belief in the empty tomb 'can be held with full intellectual integrity . . . is the understanding of the witness of Scripture which is generally received in the universal Church . . . [and expresses] the faith of the Church of England and of its historic teaching' (Para. 50).

It says of the virginal conception: 'only this belief can claim to be the teaching of the universal Church' (Para. 62). However, sadly it adds: 'On the question of whether . . . Christ's tomb that first Easter Day was empty we recognize that scholarship can offer no conclusive demonstration; and the divergent views to be found among scholars of standing are reflected in the thinking of individual bishops' (Para. 50).

'The divergences between Christian scholars on the relation of the virginal conception of our Lord to this great mystery [the incarnation], and on the question whether or not that conception is to be regarded as historical fact as well as imagery symbolic of divine truth, have been indicated, and they are reflected in the convictions of members of this House' (Para. 62).

So, for the first time ever, a report from the House of Bishops of the Church of England accepted without criticism that some of their members did not believe in the virginal conception or bodily resurrection of Christ. The saving grace is that General Synod merely 'took note of' the report so it does not have the force of law.

Sexuality and the church

By 1987 I had become increasingly concerned about laxity of sexual morals on the part of clergy, particularly in connection with homosexual practice. I had learned that there was little attempt to filter these people out at selection conference level, that one or two colleges were a hotbed of homosexual practice, and that the Dioceses of Southwark and London in particular had a considerable proportion of practising homosexual clergy. Many of these men led a promiscuous lifestyle and some enticed teenage boys into their web.

So in 1987 I put a private member's motion on sexuality to the General Synod. To be debated, a particular private member's motion has to be signed by more synod members than any other. Mine quickly reached this point and the debate was set for 11 November. Shortly before it ABWON published a booklet entitled *Sexuality and the Church*.[6] I edited it and wrote several chapters and it also included chapters by theologians and doctors. The Rev. David Holloway (Vicar of Jesmond and at that time a member of General Synod) and I launched the booklet at a press conference in a city church which a good number of media representatives attended. We circulated the booklet to all 550 General Synod members as background for the debate.

Naturally, the media (always present at the synod) took a great interest. Often only thirty minutes is allowed for a private member's motion but two hours were set aside for this debate. There were two unsuccessful attempts to torpedo the debate but, in fact, it was extended by an hour, making it equal in significance to any of the major synod debates. A wrecking amendment from the then Rector of St Botolph's, Aldgate, the church where the Lesbian and Gay Christian Movement (LGCM) had its office, was rejected by a devastating 85 per cent majority. We saw all this as an answer to the prayers of thousands of Christians around the country and elsewhere.

The wording of my original motion was:

> This synod reaffirms the biblical standard, given for the well-being of society:

1. that sexual intercourse should take place only between a man and a woman who are married to each other;
2. that fornication, adultery and homosexual acts are sinful in all circumstances;
3. that Christian leaders are called to be exemplary in all spheres of morality, including sexual morality, as a condition of being appointed to or remaining in office;

and calls upon the church to show Christ-like compassion to those who have fallen into sexual sin, encouraging them to repent and receive absolution, and offering the ministry of healing to all who suffer physically or emotionally as a result of such sin.

The House of Bishops, through Michael Baughen, then Bishop of Chester, successfully amended my wording. The wording of the amendment is not so clear; there is no reference to church discipline and it lacks reference to the ministries of absolution and healing. Initially the amendment was very weak on homosexual acts but it was, thankfully, itself amended with the addition of the words highlighted below. The final wording of the amendment, passed by a 98 per cent majority of General Synod (403 for; 8 against; 8 abstentions) was:

This Synod affirms that the biblical and traditional teaching on chastity and fidelity in personal relationships is a response to, and expression of, God's love for each one of us, and in particular affirms:

1. that sexual intercourse is an act of total commitment which belongs properly within a permanent marriage relationship;
2. that fornication and adultery are sins against this ideal, and are to be met by a call to repentance and the exercise of compassion;
3. that homosexual genital acts also fall short of this ideal, *and are likewise to be met by a call to repentance and the exercise of compassion*;
4. that all Christians are called to be exemplary in all

spheres of morality, including sexual morality, and that holiness of life is particularly required for Christian leaders.

This debate pre-empted and therefore effectively quashed an official report commissioned by the House of Bishops, which was later leaked and which proved to be disastrously liberal. So after years of sitting on the fence and being in grave danger of approving homosexual practice, the Church of England reaffirmed that fornication, adultery and homosexual acts are wrong and require repentance. It is likely that the reasonably positive outcome of that debate put back the cause of the gay lobby by ten years.

In 1997, after much prayer and discussion with my colleagues, I decided to embark on perhaps our biggest prophetic campaign ever, over the issue of homosexuality. I shall return to that in the next chapter.

Interfaith compromise

I knew in 1984 that the Lord had given me an agenda to tackle three major issues: undermining of credal belief; toleration of sexual immorality within the church, particularly in the lives of clergy; and interfaith compromise. We discovered it was important to wait for God's timing to take up each issue and resisted the insistence of others that we dealt with everything at once. One day, in May 1989, a leaflet came through the post advertising the Canterbury Festival of Faith and the Environment being organized by the International Consultancy on Religion, Education and Culture at Canterbury Cathedral in September of that year. It was clear that this would include interfaith compromise and New Age ideas.

On reading the leaflet, Patricia said she had an overwhelming conviction that this was the time to take up the issue of interfaith compromise. I shared this conviction and we found that this was a campaign which we could work on together. We wrote, for distribution at the event, an evangelistic leaflet which also warned of the dangers of New Age compromise and interfaith worship. We urged our supporters to pray and, if possible, turn up to distribute the leaflets peacefully, without causing obstruction.

But the Receiver General of the Cathedral wrote banning me from distributing any Christian evangelistic leaflet within the precincts. Yet the cathedral authorities had opened church property in and around its precincts to 'all faiths . . . to use whatever medium they may choose to express their concern for nature'. On the Friday afternoon a multifaith liturgy was held in the cathedral which excluded any reference to Jesus. On the Saturday, recruiting leaflets for other religions, including for children, were freely available.

We believe it was right to proceed, but as soon as I entered the precincts the security guards stopped me and I read their orders: 'If any members of ABWON distribute leaflets in the precincts they are to be asked to leave. If they refuse to leave the precincts you are to call the police.' We hung around the entrance, then, in the afternoon, as a final gesture, a number of us entered the precincts to distribute the evangelistic leaflets. Someone spontaneously began to sing a Christian song. We all joined in, then sang another before I said a prayer. Three guards surrounded me and said: 'Reverend Higton, by this assembly you are breaking the law. The police have been called and they are coming in force.' I have to be honest, I was tempted to stay and be arrested. But we had sensed in prayer earlier that we should make the gesture but leave when asked to do so. We gradually ambled out of the precincts and later a police van arrived – too late.

By the end of the day I felt emotionally drained and exhausted. But the unwise reaction of the authorities ensured that our campaign made the maximum impact. To this day I still find it almost incredible that cathedral authorities in England could go to such lengths to ban the peaceful distribution of evangelistic literature by a clerical General Synod member, while allowing other faiths freedom to proselytize on church land.

I discovered that the annual Commonwealth Day Observance in Westminster Abbey, in the presence of the Queen, all but excluded the name of Jesus and encouraged the worship of other so-called deities. Having failed to achieve change in this through correspondence with the Dean of Westminster, Dr Runcie and Buckingham Palace, I organized a petition to the Queen in 1990. It stated:

> While grateful for the understanding and respect between people of different nations, races and faiths fostered by the Commonwealth, nevertheless we view with deep concern and distress the multifaith nature of the worship in recent Commonwealth Day Observances in Westminster Abbey; and we believe the worship of non-Christian deities in those Observances to be incompatible with the Christian Faith; and to contradict the fundamental Christian doctrine that Jesus is the only way to God and the only Saviour. Wherefore, your Petitioners pray that your Majesty, as defender of the Faith and Visitor of Westminster Abbey, will direct that all the worship at Commonwealth Day Observances shall be specifically, explicitly and solely Christian.

It gained 77,000 signatures, but the palace let it be known to *The Times* that it was rejected by the Queen and the organizers of the Observance. However we noticed that in subsequent years the multifaith content was considerably reduced.

During 1991 Patricia and I took an initiative, involving other well-known Christian leaders, to publish an Open Letter to the leadership of the Church of England. It included the wording: 'We ... appeal to the leadership of the Church of England to oppose and, where possible, prevent such gatherings for interfaith worship and prayer in the Church of England and seek to discourage them elsewhere.'

It was circulated for signature to all the clergy and over 2000 had signed it when it was published in December 1991. The Open Letter had a major impact on the church but met with some vitriolic opposition.

One result of the Open Letter was to accelerate the publication of a General Synod Report on Multifaith Worship which was debated in July 1992. Although the treatment of biblical material was weak, this report effectively disapproved of most of the multifaith worship events ABWON has highlighted in recent years. This included the Commonwealth Day Observance. The report stated:

> It is neither appropriate nor lawful for words and actions which are contrary to the Christian Faith to be performed in an Anglican church . . . If each community is responsible for the selection and presentation of its own material, and if each brief act of worship involves what is characteristic of the faith concerned, the other communities having no implied responsibility for it, it is hard to see how such an event could be held in an Anglican church. (Para. 130)
>
> In their participation in such services, Christians should avoid giving the impression that Jesus Christ is merely one of many saviours. Christian contributors need not be embarrassed by mentioning the name of Christ. Services in which Christians participate, but in which Christ is not mentioned at all, understandably give offence to many Christians. (Para. 148)

However the relevant doctrinal statements from the Anglican formularies (The Thirty-Nine Articles of Religion) were not specified. These state that there is salvation only in the name of Christ, not in any religious practice; we are only saved through Christ, not works; works done before the grace of Christ and reception of the Holy Spirit are not pleasing to God (in the salvific sense) because they do not spring from faith in Christ.

Marginalization of Christ and justification by works are not dealt with by the Guidelines. They are also weak on idolatry.

ABWON also extensively witnessed (including through the media) in favour of sensitive evangelism of other faith groups, when Dr Carey became the first Archbishop of Canterbury in 150 years to refuse to be patron of the Church's Ministry among the Jews.

He wrote to the Society:

> Alongside my commitment to evangelism stands another commitment. It is to do all in my power to encourage trust and friendship between the different faiths in our land. The Archbishop of Canterbury is looked to as the protector of the religious freedom of people of other faiths and as a genuine friend, irrespective of the differences which separate us. I have to say that because your work is entirely directed towards another faith community, a formal association with you is unlikely to help me in my efforts to build up that trust, for rightly or wrongly, many Jewish people do not believe that CMJ respects their integrity.

In 1993 Patricia and I co-authored a book entitled *Jesus the Only Saviour*, a ten-session study course on what the Bible has to say about other faiths, people who have never heard the gospel and so on.[7] I also became involved in a number of consultations and dialogues on interfaith issues.

That year I again attended the Commonwealth Day Observance and noted how its content was now less objectionable. However Jesus was still marginalized. One reading affirmed salvation by works. Various holy books appeared to be put on a level with Scripture. The Christian reading was about ethics, not the heart of the gospel; and the assumption was made that we were all worshipping the same God.

More encouraging was the fact that in our cathedrals there was no significant multifaith compromise from the time of the Open Letter in 1991 until early 1995, when on Pentecost Sunday a Muslim was invited to preach in Christ Church Cathedral, Oxford. I protested alongside many others, particularly from Oxford Diocese.

The Open Letter was perhaps the most effective action ABWON has taken. One fifth of the clergy actively supported it, which sent shock waves around the church. It seems to have had a dramatic and long-term effect.

General prophetic witness

In February 1990, in the context of another debate on the virgin birth and bodily resurrection of Christ, I gave my toughest speech ever in synod. I ended by saying:

> The writing is on the wall for the Church of England. While we play politics in the rarefied atmosphere of this polite, exclusive religious club of General Synod, we may not notice it. If we do not put our house in order over [denials of the virgin birth and empty tomb] and other fundamental issues we shall experience great decline, great crises and great scandals, and God will give our spiritual mantle in the nation to other believers who have the courage to obey Scripture.

This prophecy was partially fulfilled in the months following, when a number of major scandals rocked the church, including some involving bishops and one an ex-General Secretary of General Synod. There was also the revelation of the massive financial losses made by the Church Commissioners in property investment to the tune of £800 million. Furthermore the number attending church continued to decline (showing just over 1 million in 1995).

In 1994 I wrote twice to the House of Bishops. The first letter urged them to public repentance over the legitimization of heresy (in their 1986 report *The Nature of Christian Belief*) and of lay homosexual practice (in their 1992 report *Issues in Human Sexuality*, to which we shall return).

It began with some positive statements and expressed gratitude for many encouragements, especially at parish level. But it went on to refer to the grave difficulties facing the church: the financial crisis; calls for disestablishment (and consequent increased marginalization of the Faith); the traumas over women priests; the lack of credibility of the church and its leadership.

The letter related this to the serious threat to all our national institutions and pointed out this is evidence of God's judgement, which always begins with the church. Finally I added that the House of Bishops was under judgement for legitimizing the heresy of those bishops and others who deny credal doctrines. And I urged the bishops to express *corporate* repentance and to put out a public statement concerning that repentance.

I did not fondly expect that the House of Bishops would publicly repent simply because I had asked them to. I do not suffer from such delusions of grandeur! Rather I was following the biblical injunction: 'Say to them, "This is what the Sovereign Lord says" . . . whether they listen or fail to listen' (Ezek. 2.4–7). But I did hope that maybe my letter would finally motivate one or two bishops to act.

Thirteen bishops replied (out of 50) but none of them expressed repentance or dissociated themselves from this legitimization of heresy. Then the Archbishop of York (John Habgood), who brought my letter to the attention of the Standing Committee of the House of Bishops, wrote saying that the committee 'had decided to take no further action'.

Because the situation was so serious, I wrote again to the bishops requesting each one to make an *individual* response to the letter either by making his own public statement or signing a form of words included in our letter. I asked each bishop specifically to:

- disassociate himself from the statements, made by those who hold teaching office in the church, denying the credal doctrines of the virginal conception of Christ and the bodily resurrection of Christ;
- disassociate himself from attempts to condone sexual immorality, whether adultery, fornication or homo-sexual practice, particularly on the part of the clergy;
- express the belief that such views are in error and should lead to anyone in an accredited teaching office in the church who persists in proclaiming or (in the case of immorality) practising them, being disciplined.

The replies were very disappointing. Eleven bishops replied but none were prepared to make the public statement I requested. Three (evangelical) bishops sent confidential replies.

(I am reminded of one diocesan bishop, now retired, who years earlier wrote to me saying his views on the virgin birth and empty tomb were confidential!) Six merely acknowledged the first letter and another four the second. Twenty-five did not reply.

Dealing with the media

Since 1984 I have given hundreds of radio, television and newspaper interviews. It is a dangerous activity. But I feel strongly that since unbiblical views and actions in the church will be picked up by an increasingly intrusive media, someone needs to speak up for biblical truth. There seem to be relatively few willing to take the risk.

I remember the first BBC TV *Newsnight* interview I gave, in 1984. I was in the studio in London and a diocesan bishop was on the line from the north of England. The interviewer asked me a question and I answered it. That was the first mistake! I learnt that it is fine briefly to answer questions. But it is important to prepare your own agenda and even wording for an interview and to hang it on the nearest question. Otherwise you only serve the purposes of an interviewer who may know little about the subject and who wants you to say things you do not regard as important or helpful.

In fact the interview had been introduced with a film in which I had been accused of publishing private responses from bishops elicited by our supporters. Because I was very green and only answered the questions, I did not actually get to say that the bishops had been asked for responses which could be made public.

The interviewer then asked the bishop a question which he proceeded to answer at great length. In those days I was not accustomed to episcopalese, the language spoken by bishops who want to sit on the fence with both ears to the ground. I could not understand what he was talking about and began to panic at the thought that the interviewer might ask me to respond to it!

This is why some bishops and clergy do not get TV air time, or at least they do not get it a second time. It is necessary to put things over in succinct plain English – sound bites, in fact. That is the nature of the medium. I am aware that it is well nigh impossible to put over some of the deeper issues of our faith in sound bites. But we shall not get opportunities to communicate to the millions in the electronic market-place unless we try.

Dealing with the media is a dangerous game. There is the danger of being deliberately misrepresented. I actually do not think that happens as often as some people claim. There is a far greater danger of being unintentionally misrepresented because of the editing down to sound bites. I have suffered a good deal from this, but I did so with my eyes open. The only way of avoiding it is not to speak to the media at all (and even then they might 'quote' you!). But I felt it was a risk I had to take, and try to minimize, to fulfil an important aspect of prophetic ministry. The great prophets of old spoke in the market-place. The media is the modern equivalent.

Another problem is that (with the exception of some serious religious documentaries) the media are only interested in *entertaining* sound bites. To be entertaining the bites have to involve confrontation or something bizarre. It is very important to realize that this is the general media approach. They will be kind and polite to you. They will make you feel important. They will flatter you. Frequently researchers have done this with me, implying I am the one person they desperately need, the only person capable of doing what they want, in fact the best thing since sliced bread. I normally respond by saying, 'Flattery will get you everywhere!' just to inform them I know I am being manipulated.

There is a grave danger of being manipulated by them into making extreme, over-confrontational or unnecessary statements in order to get on the programme and be asked back. And there is a similar danger of accepting every media invitation indiscriminately. After making a few mistakes I learnt to discriminate and have turned down many opportunities.

Never forget that the media want to use interviewees for entertainment purposes, even if it is serious entertainment. If we are going to use the media prophetically we have to meet them on that ground and play them at their own game. We shall not get opportunities if we do not please them, but the skill is to fulfil a prophetic agenda at the same time.

The Danger of Being Misunderstood

The possibilities of misunderstanding in human communication seem endless. I have often reflected that if you tell people what you are going to tell them, then tell them, then tell them what you have told them, some 50 per cent will have got the message – all being well!

If Christians do not want to be misunderstood, they should not embark on prophetic ministry. As I have already made clear, anyone taking up prophetic ministry is likely to be regarded as an unloving, narrow-minded, judgemental, brainless, fundamentalist bigot, which does not do a lot for self-esteem. The sound bite problem, together with misquotation, hearsay and gossip all conspire to undermine the prophet's credibility. I have been seriously misrepresented in many quarters – including biographies of Robert Runcie and by the *Guardian* and *Independent* in particular.

Then there is the problem of assumptions. If a prophet is hard on sin, people assume he is rejecting sinners. Sometimes people have a vested interest in making such assumptions. For example, many gay activists I have talked with refuse to accept that anyone can regard homosexual practice as sinful and not be homophobic. The old saying: 'Hate the sin, love the sinner', which admittedly can sound rather trite, is rejected and ridiculed. I can honestly say I have never hated, had a phobia about or even a gut-reaction against any homosexual, nor have I been tempted to. But such a statement will lead to peels of cynical laughter amongst my opponents. Obviously from the point of view of gay activists, only those who condone homosexual practice are loving.

We follow someone who was a 'friend of . . . sinners,' so I find it painful to be misunderstood as an enemy of sinners. The last thing I would want to do is to put off sinners from coming to Christ, which would be contrary to the gospel. Partly because I knew that people might think I was hard line against sinners, I wrote in one of the leaflets we delivered to the 12,500 people in our parish: 'Jesus welcomed all kinds of sinners. Do not misunderstand: he did not approve of sinful lifestyles, but he welcomed sinners, to help them. He still does. And so do we.' Later in the same leaflet I wrote: 'Because Jesus welcomed *everyone* we too welcome *everyone* to church, including: those with little or no faith; those totally unfamiliar with church; lone parents; those who are divorced or separated; those who have made mistakes sexually (heterosexual or homosexual); those who have messed up their lives in various ways.'

It is clear that such positive, welcoming statements are equally part of a prophetic ministry. Amidst some of the strongest condemnatory passages in the prophets are found marvellous statements about God's love, mercy and forgiveness. We shall return to this point. But the sad thing is that, in a culture which does not think in terms of sin, to prophesy against sin will cause people to think you do not believe in this welcoming side of the Faith. What you say to counteract it is likely not to be heard. A prophet must always try to bring in some aspect of God's love, mercy and forgiveness to a media interview. But it is not always possible and is likely to be edited out. I really have had to wrestle with this problem, particularly since I do not recognize myself in the public image which many have of me. But I decided I could only press on.

There is another serious danger facing those who feel called to a prophetic ministry: taking up too many issues. We look at this in the next chapter.

4 DISCERNING PROPHETIC ISSUES

In all my years on General Synod the issue on which I have received by far the most lobbying mail (other than the subjects I have majored on) is animal welfare. That is hardly surprising in our animal-loving society.

I regard ecology as a most important subject. Christians so neglected it that the high ground of the conservation movement was taken by dedicated activists who espouse New Age views. Evangelicals have only recently begun to wake up to the fact that God is Creator as well as Redeemer. He blesses his creation because he loves it, and he does so extravagantly. This is God's world and he has not called us to live in an ecclesiastical ghetto.

I have always enjoyed natural history and, in particular, ornithology. In recent years I have taken up astronomy. I am fascinated by cosmology as well as visual astronomy. Both of these hobbies relate to conservation, ornithology obviously and astronomy in that pollution, including light pollution from badly designed lighting, plays havoc with observation.

The wonders of God's creation mean a great deal to me. Similarly I feel passionately about world poverty, racism, abortion and other matters of justice. God is a God of justice and the biblical prophets thundered forth on such issues. Again many Christians, and many evangelicals, have so concentrated on personal morality that they have at times neglected the immorality of social injustice (other than abortion). However the Evangelical Alliance, under the directorship of Clive Calver, rightly began to correct this emphasis in the 1980s, seeking to follow the example of the great evangelical reformers of the last century.

But I have never taken up these issues as part of my prophetic agenda. Some will take this as proof that my comments issue from a right-wing political position (which is far from the truth). Actually, the reason is far more profound.

The Wisdom of Selection

It is vital to select prayerfully the prophetic issues it is right to take up, for various reasons. First, it is impossible for one person to take up all the important issues. The variety and complementarity God has ordained in the body of Christ mean that different prophets should take up different issues.

Second, God will not give the grace and wisdom for what I call 'uncommanded works' – good deeds God does not want us to do. We need the wisdom to distinguish good works from commanded works. The New Testament states that we are 'created in Christ Jesus to do good works, which God prepared in advance for us to do' (Eph. 2.10). We need to know which good works God has prepared for us, and to stick to them.

The church, the media, fellow-activists, our supporters and our own concerns will all conspire to lead us into uncommanded prophetic works, but we must resist it.

Over the years I have recognized the pressure to be 'doing something'. I am an activist and thrive on a challenge. I find it difficult to be inactive, but sometimes it is right to be so. For years many people have looked to me as a prophetic leader. Their expectations create pressure – the sense of obligation to be seen to be doing something. Actually, sometimes it is God's will to be seen to be doing nothing. Even the sense of needing to keep up pressure on the opposition or on ineffective church leaders has had a similar effect. I can now see others, good people who have entered the field more recently, at times succumbing to such pressures and consequently making a hash of it.

Although I stand by all the main campaigns I have undertaken, I can look back at mistakes I have made. One was over quota-capping (the capping by a parish of the voluntary annual amount it pays into the diocese). It was *The Daily Telegraph* and *Sunday Telegraph* who precipitated me into it. Out of the blue one day journalists from both papers rang and asked if our parish was capping its quota. Clearly they had been informed by someone that we were. The fact is that, facing very heavy financial demands, we were quite simply unable to pay the excessive *voluntary* quota which far exceeded anything we, as a bigger parish, cost the diocese. We were still more than paying our way, though. The papers took it as deliberate quota-capping to protest about theological and moral failure in the Church of England.

Foolishly, I allowed this to draw me into an unplanned, unintentional campaign in favour of such theological quota-capping. I have since changed my view on this matter, apart from it being a method to be used as a last resort in extreme circumstances.

Another mistake was over the issue of women priests. I have never thought that this was an issue I should take up. This is because I think Scripture is not as clear on the issue as some would have us believe and I quite understand why people sincerely interpret it differently. I also believe it to be an issue of church order rather than a primary theological matter. The ever-present ecclesiastical misogyny and chauvinism, masquerading as theology, make me profoundly unhappy, and frequently angry. And, when all is said and done, like other aspects of the church, I am content to accept women priests as a fact of life. In any case I was never opposed to their ordination, but only questioned their fulfilling certain 'headship' roles.

However, at least on one occasion, I have foolishly allowed myself to be drawn into the controversy in a way which has given the false impression I was campaigning negatively on the issue.

Christians can be deflected into pouring their time and energy into prophetic campaigns on secondary issues. I have sensed a call to witness to truths directly associated with the doctrine of salvation, such as Christology (the doctrine of Christ). This includes issues which conflict with the mission to proclaim salvation through Christ, e.g. multifaith compromise and justification of sin which the New Testament teaches will, if persisted in, hinder a person from entering the kingdom of God. These areas seem to me of fundamental importance, as opposed to such issues as the ordination of women, which I do not see as a gospel issue.

Another issue on which I have received many letters is creationism. I have written articles on cosmology and astronomy which have unintentionally rattled the cages of certain creationists. This is not the place to argue how God formed the universe. In fact such argument seems to miss the point. I really do not think the issue outside the church is *how* God created the universe but *whether* he created it. It is an eminently worthwhile campaign to try to convince people that he did create it. But the usual arguments between creationists and evolutionists seem to have the effect of further marginalizing Christian belief in God as Creator. Putting it bluntly, if people outside the church think that to believe God created the universe they must accept creation in six literal days, many will decide to reject both ideas. It is far better that they believe God did create it, whatever method they think he used, than that they should reject divine creation. If they do believe God created the universe they may well see the truth Paul teaches that 'since the creation of the world God's invisible qualities – his eternal power and divine nature – have been clearly seen, being understood from what has been made' (Rom. 1.20).

It is also important not only to choose the issues carefully but to understand the context of one's calling. Is one called to address issues mainly in the local church (or to stimulate the local church to prayer about wider issues) or to local society or the wider church or nation? My calling is specifically to prophesy in connection with the Church of England. However I have made one or two mistakes by accepting media invitations to address wider issues, e.g. moral issues which affect the nation but not the church. That is the calling of others.

The Foundation of Corporate Prayer

I always remember the elderly bishop who said, 'When the church gets stuck, it usually appoints a committee.' I am tempted to add, 'which is why it often stays stuck!' To think we can achieve God's will without much prayer is extremely arrogant. We shall not achieve God's purposes, including in prophetic ministry without prayer.

Hearing God in prayer

I am firmly of the opinion that the ideal is that the church should be a theocracy rather than a democracy. In other words, ideally it should be governed by the Lord as his people seek his guidance mainly through prayer. Such an approach is seen in the church of Antioch: 'In the church at Antioch there were prophets and teachers . . . While they were worshipping the Lord and fasting, the Holy Spirit said, "Set apart for me Barnabas and Saul for the work to which I have called them"' (Acts 13.1–2). They 'heard' God in the context of worship and prayer. This really is the only adequate foundation for a prophetic ministry.

Whatever success the prophetic ministry of ABWON has achieved is because of this. The church in Hawkwell learned to 'hear' God in prayer and the main campaigns arose from, or were confirmed through, such a theocratic approach. When I first mentioned the idea of an Open Letter on multifaith worship to our praying folk their response was positive. But they added that they felt strongly that, unlike the previous campaigns, God was calling me to work with a group of other prominent Christian leaders in setting it up, and that it should not happen under the banner of ABWON.

My inner reaction was not over-positive. I immediately thought of all the complications and extra work of getting together very busy leaders and agreeing with them precise wording and detailed procedure. However I did this because I trusted they were 'hearing' correctly. With hindsight I can see just how right they were. I would have done it differently, and probably not had the remarkable success the Open Letter had.

But how do we 'hear' God and receive his guidance?

Receiving guidance is evidence of our being children of God. It is our spiritual birthright as Christians. 'Those who are led by the Spirit of God are sons of God' (Rom. 8.14). He promises: 'I will instruct you and teach you in the way you should go; I will counsel you and watch over you' (Ps. 32.8). The Spirit of truth will guide us into all truth (John 16.13).

One of my favourite verses in Scripture is: 'If any of you lacks wisdom, he should ask God, who gives generously to all without finding fault, and it will be given to him' (Jas. 1.5). By contrast 'the wisdom of this world is foolishness in God's sight. As it is written: "He catches the wise in their craftiness"; and again, "The Lord knows that the thoughts of the wise are futile"' (1 Cor. 3.19f.).

The qualities required for 'hearing' God are first, a fear of the Lord (Ps. 25.12); second, humility (Ps. 25.9); third, a delight in the Lord for his own sake (Ps. 37.4); fourth, belief in God's promises to grant us his wisdom (compared with human wisdom: Jas. 1.5; 3.13–18); and fifth, a desire to do his will.

God uses various means to speak to us. Firstly and pre-eminently, he speaks through Scripture. But we must be careful to interpret Scripture correctly and look at all it says on a particular subject. The church will assist here. It is foolish and arrogant to ignore the teaching ministry and the tradition of the church. However, the Holy Spirit sometimes underlines a particular verse or passage of Scripture to us for illumination or guidance on a particular occasion, as I described previously when I was reading the Book of Lamentations in 1984.

Second, God uses spiritual gifts. Prophecy and the word of wisdom are relevant but care must be exercised here. These contributions must be weighed by mature Christians[1] and be in accordance with biblical teaching. Spiritual gifts are not sufficient in themselves as guidance. They must be related to and confirmed by other means of guidance.

Third, God may speak to us through dreams, visions or interpretations of dramatic circumstances.

Another means of 'hearing' God is an 'inner peace' or what some Christians call a 'witness of the Spirit' that some course of action is right. But it is peace with God – a peace which draws us closer to God. Again, this must be related to and confirmed by other means of guidance.[2]

More frequently God speaks to us through that inner prompting, the gentle whisper of the Spirit, a deep conviction in one's spirit, as described when we believed it right to proceed with the interfaith campaign (having previously felt a hesitation, a sense that prior to that occasion in 1989 it was not the right time). The main way God has guided me over prophetic action has been through what I can only describe as an overwhelming sense of obligation which is not removed until I have decided on a course of action.

Last, God 'speaks' through the advice of others (Prov. 12.15). The New Testament knows nothing of the isolated Christian living by 'hot-line' guidance from God. Church history is littered with such people coming to grief. Their attitude is one of arrogance. The New Testament teaches that much guidance comes through the body of Christ to the individual. So God will sometimes guide through the ministry of church leaders (Heb. 13.17). At other times prayerful discussion with others will provide guidance.[3]

Intercession

It is evident that the great biblical prophets were men of prayer. Elijah prophesied to King Ahab: 'As the Lord, the God of Israel, lives, whom I serve, there will be neither dew nor rain in the next few years except at my word' (1 Kings 17.1). And the drought happened. Three and a half years later he prophesied to Ahab that the Lord would send rain. And the drought ended. But the secret of Elijah's success is given by James: 'Elijah was a man just like us. He prayed earnestly that it would not rain, and it did not rain on the land for three and a half years. Again he prayed, and the heavens gave rain, and the earth produced its crops' (Jas. 5.17f.).

When confronted by the might of Sennacherib, Hezekiah, in desperation, sent his officials to Isaiah asking him to 'pray for the remnant that still survives'. Isaiah delivered a powerful prophecy to Hezekiah predicting Sennacherib's downfall. But it is important to note that both Hezekiah and Isaiah also 'cried out in prayer to heaven about this' (2 Chron. 32.20).

Zedekiah, made King of Judah by Nebuchadnezzar of Babylon, urged Jeremiah to pray for him and the people. Similarly, after the assassination of Gedaliah, the governor appointed by Babylon, the leaders of Judah approached Jeremiah and said: '"Please hear our petition and pray to the Lord your God for this entire remnant. For as you now see, though we were once many, now only a few are left. Pray that the Lord your God will tell us where we should go and what we should do." "I have heard you," replied Jeremiah the prophet. "I will certainly pray to the Lord your God as you have requested; I will tell you everything the Lord says and will keep nothing back from you"' (Jer. 42.2–4). It was only ten days later, during which, no doubt, Jeremiah prayed earnestly, that the word of the Lord came to him for the situation.

Jeremiah points out the reason for the failure of the false prophets. He asks, 'Which of them has stood in the council of the Lord to see or to hear his word? Who has listened and heard his word?' He adds: 'if they had stood in my council, they would have proclaimed my words to my people and would have turned them from their evil ways and from their evil deeds' (Jer. 23.18, 22).

At this point I want to pay tribute to the hundreds of Christians who have consistently prayed for me in my prophetic role. Wherever I go in this country, and also overseas, people come up to me to thank me for taking a stand, for being a voice for the person in the pew, and many assure me they pray for me regularly. I find this very humbling and know this ministry would have made little impact without that support.

Current Issues

The reason why the media successfully focuses on the bad news is because that suits public interest; and that attitude is shared by many Christians. However it can, of course, give a very unbalanced picture of the real situation in the church. There are some serious problems currently facing the Church of England, but there are also encouragements.

The bad old days

The 1980s and early 1990s were a dark time for the Church of England. It was a time when a hard-line and manipulative liberalism had gained the ascendancy, represented in the outlook of the two archbishops. I want to add immediately that I recognized a change in John Habgood in his final years in York. Earlier he had come over as a brilliant but hard-line, rather condescending, liberal. But he mellowed considerably. I was impressed by the sensitive way he piloted the women priests issue through the General Synod and, having been one of his fiercest critics, I took the opportunity to thank him for it.

I wish I could say the same for Robert Runcie. But I cannot. It is true that he showed a deep concern for social issues. He piloted *Faith in the City* through the synod. And during those years the church was the only effective opposition to the government. Some Christians disagreed with the church's stance on social and political issues but no one could deny that it was seeking to fulfil its prophetic role in that respect.

But basically, I still regard Robert Runcie's archiepiscopate as a disaster for the Church of England. Those who may think, in this improved situation in the late 1990s, that some of us were 'over the top' in our criticisms in the Runcie era are probably suffering from short memories or were not in the thick of things in the 1980s. Although there were imperfections in my approach, I do not regret anything of significance in my outspoken opposition during that era. In fact I rather feel that the main reason God called me to direct the ministry of ABWON was to be a prophetic voice to the Church of England, in that dark decade.

During it, for the first time ever, the hierarchy effectively legitimized episcopal denial of credal doctrine. Also tacit and hypocritical encouragement was given to the gay lobby to begin to recover from its major defeat in the 1987 General Synod debate. And multifaith worship which marginalized or excluded Jesus and proclaimed doctrines contrary to the gospel (even involving actual worship of other gods in church buildings) began to grow apace. Yes, there were days of exhilaration of battle for some of us, but most would want to draw a veil over that period in the history of the Church of England

Improvements in the 1990s

However, the situation has changed, even though some people have not noticed. One is reminded of those poor Second World War soldiers discovered years after the war had ended, still hiding in the jungles of South East Asia in the belief that the conflict continued. It would be a serious overstatement to say the conflict in the church is over. But some things have improved.

We now have two archbishops who are godly men with the proclamation of the gospel on their hearts and a high view of Scripture. We have many similar men in the House of Bishops, far more than in the 1980s.

Recent doctrinal reports considered by General Synod, whatever their weaknesses, have been far more biblical than some of those in the previous decade. I find it difficult to imagine that the Durham Controversy would occur in the near future – namely the appointment as bishop of a cleric who had already publicly denied credal doctrine.

After the 1990 Open Letter against multifaith worship signed by 2010 clergy (one fifth of the total) I am not aware that any such damaging events have taken place. The only exception was the invitation to a Muslim to preach at the Pentecost service in Christ Church, Oxford. But that appears to have been an isolated incident.

There is even some good news on the matter of homosexuality. The 1987 debate on my Private Member's Motion (which re-established the official, traditional view on sexuality) set back the cause of the gay activists by some years. The appalling Osborn Report, a product of the 1980s commissioned by the House of Bishops in 1986, had it been published, would have done enormous damage to the church. It was, in effect, ousted by the 1987 resolution, but I saw a 'leaked' copy (courtesy of Granada Television). By comparison *Issues in*

Human Sexuality, the 1991 bishops' report which replaced the Osborn Report is pretty conservative (although seriously flawed). I believe there is little likelihood of any official acceptance of practising homosexual clergy within the foreseeable future, and that is confirmed by numerous private communications I have had from bishops. Nevertheless there is real cause for concern over this issue as we shall see in Chapter 8.

The church has also began during this Decade of Evangelism to move, painfully slowly, from a maintenance to mission outlook. Instead of simply existing to maintain the status quo, some parishes are just beginning to realize they have a mission responsibility, and others are taking active steps to do something about that. The widespread use of the Alpha Course for enquirers has been a remarkable phenomenon.[4]

The financial constraints of the present decade have led to some hard rethinking about structures and priorities, although there is a long way to go.

So there is much cause for thanksgiving as we compare the 1990s with the previous decade. And we ought not to deprive the Lord of thanksgiving, or his people of encouragement, by allowing the current problems to blot it out.

Present challenges

However (and it is an important 'however') the price of freedom (from unbiblical views and practices) is eternal vigilance. And, in any case, there are still some blatant faults in the church.

It may be true that the Durham Controversy is not likely to be repeated. But since the bishops' 1986 report *The Nature of Christian Belief* effectively legitimized the views David Jenkins espoused, the more subtle danger is of a doctrinal drift. In November 1996 the General Synod sadly decided in principle against including doctrinal issues in the new clergy discipline procedures, rather leaving them to current procedures. It was easy to get hold of the Durham Controversy because it was overt and public. The current danger is more slippery. It can only be dealt with by prayer, prophetic warning and action such as ensuring the training of ordinands is intelligently biblical, and that doctrinal questions are asked of candidates prior to ordination.

A watching brief also needs to be maintained on the interfaith front. The current silence should not lull us into a false sense of security. The Prince of Wales, the next Supreme Governor on earth of the Church of England, is clearly uncritically pro-Islam. He also holds some rather New Age, syncretistic views. His influence should not be underestimated. It is also likely that we shall see syncretistic services or events planned to celebrate the millennium. George Carey is a good archbishop, who deserves our prayerful, though not uncritical, support. I affirm so much of what he has already achieved in his time in office. Nevertheless, his views on interfaith matters continue to cause concern. His refusal to be patron of the Church's Ministry among the Jews, which I have discussed with him more than once, gave all the wrong signals. I applaud his concern to establish good relations and foster co-operation over social and moral issues between the various faith communities, and to counteract racism and prejudice. But that must never be at the cost of compromising the gospel or hindering people from embracing it. I am sure Dr Carey would agree with that, but I nevertheless question the wisdom of various statements he has made on the subject. We must remain alert to the fact that interfaith compromise could raise its head once more.

There is a drift, similar to that in doctrinal matters, in the area of homosexual practice which can only be dealt with in the same way. Speaking of a homosexual lifestyle the bishops' report *Issues in Human Sexuality* states: 'While unable therefore to commend the way of life just described as in itself as faithful a reflection of God's purposes in creation as the heterosexual, we do not reject those who sincerely believe it is God's call to them, we stand alongside them in the fellowship of the church, all alike dependent upon the undeserved grace of God.' It continues: 'Candidates for ordination also must be prepared to abide by the same standards. For reasons already mentioned, however, we do not think it right to interrogate individuals on their sexual lives. Ordinarily it should be left to the candidates' own consciences to act responsibly in this matter' (Paras 5.6 and 5.22).

I would like to interpret the report as only welcoming homosexual couples to attend church, rather than allowing them to take communion or to be appointed to lay leadership. But, in all honesty I cannot do so. Even Michael Baughen, who, as Bishop of Chester, fought against the pro-homosexual tide in the 1980s, interpreted it as 'not normally' allowing such people into leadership!

Then there was the Lesbian and Gay Christian Movement's (LGCM) anniversary service in Southwark Cathedral in 1996, approved by one evangelical bishop and preached at by another. In allowing such an event the cathedral authorities were guilty of supporting that which is contrary to basic Christian morality. They trampled on the conscientious feelings of many clergy and laity in Southwark Diocese and elsewhere. No tolerance, understanding and fairness was shown to them, even though hundreds protested. The consequences are most serious. Reasonable representations having been rejected, I consider churches to be justified in taking sanctions against the cathedral.

LGCM will press for other such events and the precedent with its weak arguments about cathedral hospitality will undermine the case for other cathedrals refusing. But they must do so or be made to face very serious consequences (of financial sanctions, churches boycotting use of cathedrals, etc.). Even though it is unlikely that the Church of England will officially change its stance on homosexual practice in the next decade, I think it is a scandal that there are practising homosexual clergy, known to bishops, who are not disciplined.

It was because of all this that we launched our 1997 national campaign concerning homosexual practice. We circulated to all 10,000 full-time clergy in England a study booklet for clergy and leaders and a popular study course for church members together with advice on action local church councils could take over the issue. The materials not only referred to Scripture but also to *Issues in Human Sexuality*.[5] The campaign was an act of faith. It cost £13,000 but we only had £3,000 capital in ABWON. I thank God that within weeks the full amount had come in from donations.

The idea was to provide the resources for an informed (but not fundamentalist or homophobic) response from the grass roots. We wanted to give a voice to those who felt no one would listen to them. We gave permission to churches to photocopy these resources freely.

We encouraged church councils to pass resolutions calling for the church to retain the biblical position on homosexual practice and to send copies of them to their bishops, archbishop and General Synod representatives. The mailing went out a couple of months before the July 1997 General Synod debated a private member's motion commending *Issues in Human Sexuality* for study in the dioceses, deaneries and parishes.

At the time of writing, it is too early for the full results of this campaign to be clear but many churches have passed the relevant motion. It surely cannot be a coincidence that three weeks after the mailing went out, amidst a blaze of national publicity, the House of Bishops took the unprecedented step of issuing a statement that they would resist any amendment to the fairly innocuous motion before the synod. They carried out their intention and so prevented the pro-gay lobby from hijacking the debate. They also issued a statement, for the first time in ten years, reaffirming the 1987 resolution as the official position of the Church of England. This, together with good speeches from both archbishops upholding traditional morality, ensured the debate (contrary to some media reports and gay propaganda) did not move the church in a pro-gay direction, for which we praise God.

Other issues the church (and prophetic people) must face include the overemphasis on episcopal collegiality which can lead to placing unity above truth; the need for even greater financial realism in the church and the obligation for each church to practise rather than merely discuss mission.

It is good that the House of Bishops seeks to maintain unity and speaks with one voice. But experience shows the danger of this leading them to 'speak with forked tongue'. Unity is not an agreed form of words which is so planned that it can be interpreted in totally contradictory ways by different people. Nor is the welfare of the church furthered by agreeing to reports which contain serious errors 'because it was the best we could achieve'. That is fine over secondary issues, but not over basic doctrine or morality. I recently heard a wonderful example of episcopal thinking on this. It went like this: 'If we conservatives break ranks [over *Issues in Human Sexuality*, etc.] the radicals will also break ranks. If we don't, they won't.' Am I the only person to think this convoluted thinking would not have commended itself to the apostles, or more important, to Jesus?

I am all in favour of collegiality, within biblical limits. But, according to Canon C18, bishops are not only 'to teach and uphold sound and wholesome doctrine', they are also biblically and legally obliged 'to banish and drive away all erroneous and strange opinions'. They should be encouraged to do so where necessary.

Then there is the need for financial realism in the church. Economies are being made and structures are being streamlined. But what is God saying through our financial straits? He is surely calling the church to face up to reality. We cannot maintain a system where many churches are being subsidized. The only answer is for the vast majority of churches to become financially self-supporting (even if their finances are channelled through the diocese). But the real point is that, apart from in exceptional circumstances, the churches which are proclaiming and living the gospel, basing their lives on prayer and biblical teaching, discovering and using the gifts of every member in the unity and power of the Spirit, develop enough to be self-supporting. The purpose of and answer to our financial difficulties is for parishes to realize this. For dioceses merely to make economies and to reorganize, shields churches from reality and so does them a great disservice. I believe God intends our financial problems to bring us to our knees – in prayer. We have not yet got the message.

Finally, the prophets must call the church to get beyond

acknowledging that mission should be on our agenda and even putting it on our agenda. We need a paradigm shift whereby we begin to live for those outside the church and, in so doing, to live for God. We must think, plan *and act* practically, critically and creatively about mission. This includes social concern, bridge-building but also direct evangelism. Many Christians do not evangelize because they do not know what to say. Mission requires the work of the Spirit, but this is not negated by training programmes which help people to know what to say, how to say it and how to make opportunities for witnessing. Churches must be equipped with such programmes together with materials and resources for nurture groups and discipleship groups. Happily there is now a plethora of such resources available to the church.

One of the factors which gave me strength in the first ten years of my prophetic ministry was that I was rooted and grounded in a thriving church, which reached out with the love of Christ to the world. Not only that, but prophetically ahead of it being acceptable, my wife spearheaded a ministry encouraging hundreds of other churches to be 'Together for Intercession, Ministry and Evangelism' (hence the acrostic 'TIME' in Time Ministries International, the organization we founded and direct). Based upon our experience in our own parish we have produced resources which have been used to encourage 1000 churches to date in every-member ministry. The *Called to Serve* course we wrote, which is fundamental to these resources, has sold almost 40,000 copies.[6] The prophetic message is that mission is not a means of solving our financial difficulties and it is not a mere agenda item – it is essential to being the church.

These then are some of the main prophetic challenges facing us in the church: combating relativism in basic doctrine and sexual morality; resisting any return to interfaith compromise; calling for an end to unhelpful episcopal collegiality; pointing to what God is saying through our financial difficulties and proclaiming mission and evangelism to be part of the essential nature of the church.

Prophesy to society

This book is concentrating on prophetic ministry within the church and to the church, but that cannot be isolated from the church's solemn obligation to prophesy to society. After all, one of the most important reasons for prophesying to the church is so that we put our own house in order so as to be really effective in our ministry to society.

From time to time church leaders such as Dr Carey have called upon society to return to basic moral standards, only to be criticized by conservative Christians who say that society needs the gospel, not morality. They add that without the gospel there will be no return to morality anyway.

Obviously, this country primarily needs the gospel which centres on the justification of repentant sinners through trust in Christ. God 'is not wanting anyone to perish, but everyone to come to repentance' (2 Pet. 3.9). So, second to worship, evangelism is the church's priority. But that is not all the nation needs.

God richly, even extravagantly, blesses human beings, believers and unbelievers, righteous and unrighteous. He places them in a beautiful world; inspires artistic, musical and creative talents; prompts love and self-sacrifice. These actions are not *directly* related to the work of redemption, except in the sense that God seeks to win people to repentance through his kindness. In other words, God spends a lot of his time and energy blessing human beings simply because he loves them. So should we.

Then God has provided marriage and the family – creation ordinances simply for the benefit of the individual and society. He has also provided governing authorities, law and order for human benefit. Again, none of these is *directly* related to the work of redemption.

Similarly, God has provided the Maker's Instructions (the Ten Commandments and other laws) for the benefit of humanity, not only to be a means of bringing people to Christ. They are good in themselves, not only in relationship to redemption. And we are right to call people back to the Maker's loving instructions for an ordered life, for the benefit of society.

God doesn't only love the church: he loves the world!

So it is godly to bless unbelievers and to work for their welfare, including calling them back to the Maker's Instructions. It is also godly to long that they will come to faith and be saved. But, as the healing ministry of Jesus shows, the danger is that people will accept the benefits and reject the one who gives them. Jesus took that risk – so should we. In any case, blessing unbelievers and explaining the benefits of God's laws forms a good foundation for evangelism.

There is no place in this book to examine the current issues I believe the church ought to be taking up prophetically in society. But the biblical teaching on justice issues indicates an agenda. In particular it stresses how important it is for the church to be concerned and vigilant about the way society treats people, especially the poor, weak and vulnerable.

Scripture teaches that God is a God of justice; he loves justice. The kingdom of God, established through Christ, is a kingdom of love, faithfulness, justice and righteousness. He will bring justice to the nations and particularly to the poor. He defends, sustains and secures justice for the fatherless, widows, alien, oppressed, weak, needy and poor.[7]

God hates injustice, oppression, extortion, dispossession, dishonest business, bribery and commands us to avoid them.[8] He commands us to defend the rights of the weak, needy, fatherless, poor and oppressed; to rescue them and administer justice.[9] Under Old Testament law the poor are to be provided with food, not to be charged interest or sold food at a profit. Their debts may be cancelled.[10]

God watches over aliens (foreigners, people from another tribe, race, social or religious background) and condemns those who ill-treat or withhold justice from them. All human beings are equal in God's sight (Gen. 1.26–27; Gal. 3.28). He commands us to love the aliens as ourselves, to treat them as our native-born and help them where necessary (Lev. 19.33f.). Even the offender is to have humane punishment and is not to be degraded (Deut. 25.2f.).

God has given human beings responsibility for creation, so they are to care for the environment (Gen. 1.28; 2.15).

Consequently, the church is right to be at the forefront of prophetic proclamation and action about such issues as national and world poverty; racism and tribalism; social division and violence; immigration and asylum seekers; religious, political and economic oppression; dishonest and unjust business; unjust laws and punishments; injustice in society and the judiciary; conservation and animal welfare.

Our own church sends money regularly to a famine relief organization, supports two missions to persecuted Christians and will get involved in the Jubilee 2000 campaign to cancel Third World debts. The congregation at our parish church majors on ministry to the needy and bereaved.

The provisos are, though, that we put our own house in order as a matter of urgent priority; that we do our homework on the issues and that we each follow our particular calling. Not all prophets are called to prophesy to society, and those who are should prayerfully select their subjects.

5 *PROPHESYING IN FAITH*

There are too many square pegs in round holes within the church. Because of the job description for clergy sometimes evangelists have to major on pastoral work, prophets on teaching and pastors on evangelism. Then, on occasions, we appoint administrators to the apostolic role of a bishop, and we wonder why it does not work too effectively. The fact that it works as well as it does is one of the great evidences that the age of miracles is not over! But it could work much better.

God's intention through the charismatic renewal was not simply to liven up the worship with repetitive chorus-singing! It has a profoundly theological purpose – to call the church back to the New Testament norm of being charismatic in its ministerial structure. God has taken the trouble to give different gifts and we need to set people free to major on their gift(s). That is not to say we should not also be involved in ministries for which we are not gifted. That is simply impractical idealism; and it can lead to what I might call 'charismatic selfishness' where individuals will not lift a finger to help with urgent ministerial needs outside the sphere in which they are gifted.

However, if we do not firmly aim to be charismatic in this ecclesiological sense we shall not achieve our full potential and life-purpose in ministry. The New Testament is quite clear that the various different manifestations of the Spirit are for the common good of the church (1 Cor. 12.7; cf. 14.26). Input from the leading ministries of apostle, prophet, evangelist, pastor and teacher are essential for preparing God's people for works of service, for building up the body of Christ in unity, knowledge and maturity (Eph. 4.7–13). Peter makes it clear that 'Each one should use whatever gift he has received to serve others, faithfully administering God's grace in its various forms' (1 Pet.

4.10). So those who sense God has given them a gift of prophecy should take it seriously. The norm is that this should be confirmed by those in authority within the church. This is important for the protection of the individual from error and for good order in ministry within the church.

There is, though, another important consideration. Not only should we major on ministering according to our gift(s), but also according to our faith. Paul writes to the Romans: 'We have different gifts, according to the grace given us. If a man's gift is prophesying, let him use it in proportion to his faith' (Rom. 12.6).

Just because someone genuinely has a gift of prophecy does not mean God has called that person to prophesy in every context and on every subject. Experience teaches that there will be a specialization within the specialization. The prophet must ask in what context and on what subject(s) God has given him or her the faith to prophesy.

Some are called to exercise a prophetic ministry to individuals, bringing specific words of encouragement and challenge from God. Others are called, and have the faith, to exercise a prophetic ministry, bringing God's 'now' word to a congregation. There are those who are involved in the leadership team of a church who exercise a prophetic ministry discerning the next step for that church to take. Such prophecy may take the form of imparting vision or sharing insights within discussions and conversations (perhaps for others to act on). It is not always a 'set piece' in some self-conscious, prophetic format. Rather it appears more incidental, but nevertheless inspiring and effective.

Whereas such people may well have insights about the wider church, it is important that these are turned into prayer rather than direct prophecy, unless one's level of faith deepens and one has a clear sense of call to convey the message publicly.

Those with prophetic insight about the local or the wider church, but no sense of call to discharge a prophetic ministry, can usefully channel their discernment in the context of corporate prayer, assuming there is opportunity for participants to convey what they believe the Holy Spirit is saying. The best prayer gatherings are those where the participants have prophetic understanding of the bigger picture (whether international, national, wider church, denomination, etc., depending on the topic) and against that background can home in on the more particular matter which God is highlighting for that occasion.

Anyone who believes God may be calling them to take up a prophetic ministry to their denomination or even wider than that, should seriously weigh up the following considerations, some of which I have already touched on.

Be sure of your calling. A prophetic ministry is a difficult calling, so it is essential that you have a strong sense of call. The call should include biblical content – God speaking to you through Scripture about the need to take up prophetic ministry.

It should also include a strong sense of obligation to prophesy. Do not do it unless you can do no other. The great biblical prophets spoke of this. Amos said, 'The Sovereign Lord has spoken – who can but prophesy?' (Amos 3.8). Jeremiah expressed it more graphically: 'But if I say, "I will not mention him or speak any more in his name," his word is in my heart like a fire, a fire shut up in my bones. I am weary of holding it in; indeed, I cannot' (Jer. 20.9).

The call should also be confirmed by mature leaders believing you have a prophetic gift, a prophetic calling and will develop a prophetic ministry.

It is also good from time to time to lay your calling before God seeking confirmation that it is right to continue and checking if a mid-course correction is required.

Count the cost. There will be a cost to your reputation. In fact you will need to lay down your reputation. I have described that from my own experience, but it is far better illustrated in the ministry of Jesus, John the Baptist and the Old Testament prophets.

If you are hoping for acceptability, commendation, popularity or promotion, do not pursue the prophetic ministry. We follow someone who made himself of no reputation and they crucified him.

Beware also being wrongly influenced by the reputation a prophetic ministry gains with others who are prophetic, or with those who are critical of the same issues as yourself. Lay that down too. It is necessary to reaffirm the laying down of reputation from time to time.

There will be a cost to family life as well. Sometimes it is more painful to see your loved one suffering strong, even vitriolic criticism than to experience such criticism yourself. My wife has found it quite difficult to read or hear very public, unjust criticisms of me. However, she is fully supportive, which is vital in such a ministry. It is even better if you both have prophetic understanding and can work together to some extent, which has been the case for us.

Then there is the cost to existing ministry. The research and preparation for a prophetic ministry take much time. The meetings, phone calls and correspondence add considerably to this. We were able to delegate extensively in our parish, making it possible to spend time on ABWON. In addition, misunderstanding and loss of reputation will have an effect on existing ministry. For example, if your false image is of a narrow-minded, legalistic bigot, it hardly helps to build confidence in you on the part of parishioners who do not attend church! That is one of the side-effects that I have taken most seriously. One must take the way of faith – in our case, when the ministry of ABWON was most effective, at that time so was the parochial ministry.

Check your attitudes. It is important to aim to show true (biblical) love which includes both 'kindness and sternness' (Rom. 11.22). One must seek after love, joy, peace, patience, goodness, faithfulness, gentleness and self-control, humility, compassion, forgiveness, mercy, sincerity, purity and impartiality. It is important to honour others above oneself; to be peace-loving, considerate and encouraging. Those who know me know how far short I fall of some of these qualities, so thank God that he does use imperfect people.

We must not use our defence of prophetic sternness to

justify behaviour which conflicts with a truly biblical and Christ-like definition of love. We should avoid selfish anger, rebellion, argumentativeness, judgementalism, a critical spirit, personal antagonism and rudeness, quarrelling, slander, gossip and arrogance.

Prophetic sternness must not lead to rebellion against authority. A proper respect for authority and submission where biblical principles are upheld is a biblical injunction. We are not called to be rebels.

Know how to deal with opposition and hurts. Learn how to rejoice in suffering (Rom. 5.3–5) and to bless those who hurt you (Rom. 12.12). Do not harbour resentment (1 Cor. 13.4–5). The most important thing you can do for your opponents and those whose actions you oppose is to pray for them which will keep your attitude towards them positive. Some people who claim to be prophetic seem almost to hate those they are confronting. Never forget: 'If I have the gift of prophecy . . . but have not love, I am nothing' (1 Cor. 13.2).

Ensure you have united corporate prayer-backing. You need at least a fair-sized group of mature leaders who know what it is to intercede in depth, to 'hear' God and who are unafraid to correct you. These may be members of your local church.

It is essential that your corporate prayer/support base is deeply united. Otherwise its intercession, spiritual warfare and 'hearing' God will be seriously undermined. Also Satan would be able to wreak havoc if it were disunited. One cannot be effective in the war against heresy and failure in the wider church if one has the danger or actual experience of civil war in the home base.[1] This group should be able to keep confidences and may also act as an advisory body (depending on their maturity). However the Lord may provide, as he did in our case, a much wider, more diverse company of prayer supporters.

Ensure you are rooted in a local church. It is vital that you are rooted in a local church which can care for you, pray for you and correct you. Another reason for this is so that you are not isolated from the other ministries: pastoral, evangelistic and teaching. This is important in maintaining a balance in ministry.

Take steps of faith. Your faith and ability to minister prophetically will develop. The Lord will prepare you for more demanding prophetic action. I vividly remember my baptism of fire. A few weeks after my call to prophetic ministry in February 1984 I read a report in a national newspaper that a clergyman in our diocese, who was prominent in what was then called the Gay Christian Movement, had been made canon by our bishop. The bishop had not intended this to commend his views on homosexual practice but, inevitably, the press took it that way.

As I read the article I had a sinking feeling in my stomach. I knew this was it. I had got to burn my bridges and speak out about it. The prospect of confrontation with this man and my bishop was painful (and threatening). I conveyed my disapproval to the bishop and my stand against the appointment became public. The local press informed me they were going to ask for more details.

One morning, just before a church member was due to see me, the editor of the local paper rang me. He told me they had discovered the clergyman in question was very seriously ill and they were dubious about commenting on the matter. I felt dreadful. I had felt bad enough taking the action in the first place. I shall never forget sitting there after the phone call gazing through the study window for an hour or more. Patricia had to deal with the church member on her own. She said afterwards that I looked shocked and ill. 'What have I done?' I thought. 'Is it all a horrible mistake?' I began to pray, 'Lord, have I mistaken your call? Have I stepped out of your will? Will it all be disastrously counterproductive? Shall I try and stop the whole protest?'

Eventually, still feeling awful, I decided that in all conscience I could not back down. Later I learnt that the clergyman in question was not as seriously ill at that time as I had been told. I also discovered that his views on sexual morality were far more serious than I had known. Over the next few weeks I received much hard evidence that confirmed the rightness of my stand.

I believe God allowed this as my baptism of fire to prepare me for much bigger prophetic actions to come.

Pray for and about opportunities to be prophetic. It is important to be clear about the sphere of your calling as we discussed above. It is also vital prayerfully to choose your battles. God has prepared good works in advance for us to do (Eph. 2.10). We must therefore only fight those battles God wants us to. People will seek to involve us in other campaigns. All we do must be conceived in (corporate) prayer and 'hearing' God. Once we are clear, we should actively look for opportunities to prophesy and even be pro-active (as I was with the General Synod motion on sexuality). At other times opportunities will come 'out of the blue'.

Consider the medium for the message. Is God calling you to write a book or an article, to produce a magazine, to preach, to be involved in synods, to look for openings in the secular media, to write prophetic drama or music, to take prophetic action e.g. against social evils? Or is he calling you to 'come in the opposite spirit' by seeking to develop unity when the evil is division, and so on?

Check your facts. Major on researching the relevant subjects and keeping up to date. It is wrong to misrepresent your opponents, so gain reliable information on their words and actions.

Be positive where possible. It is important, where possible, to be positive about the church or nation or about the people you criticize. This will help keep your attitude positive and maintain a sense of balance. It also gives credit where it is due and properly commends your ministry.

Be aware of Satan's strategy. Without falling into the Christian superstition of seeing demons everywhere (especially where there are none), it is important to remember the reality of spiritual warfare. Watch your back! If the devil can hinder or stop your prophetic witness by subtle temptations and attacks, he will. On the very night I preached my first major prophetic sermon, I discovered that a leader in our church had been engaging in seriously divisive action within our parish. I had to spend much time and energy sorting out the situation.

Maintain your spiritual life. A lack of personal holiness will undermine and hinder a prophetic ministry; and it will render a person vulnerable to satanic attack.

Research and keep up to date with relevant theology. All those involved in prophetic ministry, even on a personal and minor level within the local church need to increase their knowledge of Scripture in order to mature and purify their ministry. All prophecy must be checked by Scripture so the more knowledge of Scripture a person involved in prophetic ministry has the better.

For those with a more prominent prophetic ministry it is vital that they have done critical study of the relevant theological and biblical issues so that they convey thoughtful, scriptural comments. This will help prevent serious weaknesses developing in the ministry. It will also help avoid mistakes which undermine the credibility of the prophetic ministry.

However it is little use seeking to be prophetic if we are doing so in the wrong way and with sinful attitudes which speak so loudly that they drown out our message. It is to this aspect that we turn in the next chapter.

6 'PROPHETIC' DEVIATIONS – THE DOOM AND GLOOM BRIGADE

Some years ago one of our leaders asked to speak to me privately. She felt God had given her an important prophetic message for a couple in her housegroup. She had conveyed it to them and they had rejected it, creating distress all round. But she still felt the message was a genuine prophecy.

When she told me what the message was, I too felt it was genuine, accurate and appropriate to the couple concerned. In fact I felt it was an important and helpful message. Why then had they, as people familiar with the gift of prophecy, rejected it?

Initially, I was stumped and breathed a silent prayer for help. Then it came to me. I asked, 'As you conveyed the message to them, how did you feel towards them?' She thought for a time, then replied, 'Well, if I am honest, I felt rather irritated with them.' 'That is why it went wrong,' I said, 'It was a genuine prophecy, but you did not convey it in love.'

The Supremacy of Love

Paul makes it quite clear: 'If I have the gift of prophecy . . . but have not love, I am nothing' (1 Cor. 13.2). He refers to other gifts of the Spirit – tongues, the message of wisdom, the message of knowledge, faith – as well as sacrificial giving and martyrdom, and says that they must all be done in love (1 Cor. 13.1–3).

He then goes on to speak prophetically to prophets and would-be prophets, among many others: 'Love is patient, love is kind. It does not envy, it does not boast, it is not proud. It is not rude, it is not self-seeking, it is not easily angered, it keeps no record of wrongs. Love does not delight in evil but rejoices with the truth. It always protects, always trusts, always hopes, always perseveres' (1 Cor. 13.4–7).

However, it is all too possible for prophets to fail to show these qualities. There is a proper prophetic sense of urgency about correcting the failings in the church so that it may get on with the task of mission. But there is also an ungodly impatience with those who are slow to change, or unhelpful attitudes to those who resist change.

We have seen that there is a place for strong language as Jesus and the apostles showed. Kindness does not mean being consistently soft and inoffensive. But it does mean having a positive attitude towards those being criticized as people. It does mean speaking positively when possible.

Whereas Paul taught rudeness must be avoided, he certainly used colourful language against his opponents when the gospel and the welfare of the church were at stake.[1] Jesus and the apostles also displayed righteous anger. This is a genuinely unselfish quality. But there is always the danger of unrighteous, selfish anger entering into a prophetic ministry.

Prophets have to address the faults of the church and they will tend to be rejected for doing so. It is essential then that they do not keep a resentful record of personal hurts inflicted upon them during the course of their ministry. Given the ability of some Christians who accuse prophets of being unloving, to be more unloving than those they criticize, this is important teaching!

So, in focusing on the importance of loving attitudes, we must remember that the New Testament shows there is a place for strong language and righteous anger. But there is also a vital place for patience, kindness and forgiveness, without which any ministry will be undermined and even damaging.

But that is not all. In this passage, Paul also teaches that we must avoid delighting in evil and ignoring what is good in the situation. He says we must avoid cynical distrust of people and never finally give them up as a dead loss. This brings us directly into conflict with the Doom and Gloom Brigade.

Biblical Doom and Gloom

A truly biblical prophetic ministry will stress both the positive and the negative; the encouragements and the discouragements; the commendation and the condemnation; the mercy and the judgement.

God is love. He is infinitely kind, gentle, merciful and forgiving. He wants his children to experience 'inexpressible joy' and the peace that transcends understanding. He is the redeemer, healer, restorer and deliverer.

However he is also the judge of the whole earth. Scripture speaks of his sternness as well as his kindness (Rom. 11.22). Jesus and the New Testament writers clearly believe in the wrath of God. 'Wrath' is a human word applied to God. With him it is not a selfish, irrational passion. Rather it is the reaction of God's holiness against sin.

The Book of Revelation foretells divine judgement through famine, plague, cosmic disturbance and earthquakes (Rev. 7–9, 15–16). Some 60 per cent of Revelation, which refers to itself as a prophecy (Rev. 1.3; 22.18f.), is 'doom and gloom'. There are similar passages in 2 Thessalonians 1–2 and 2 Peter 2–3.

Over 80 per cent of Old Testament prophecy is 'doom and gloom'. The prophets were sent to warn God's people.[2] They were sent again and again to urge them to turn away from their sin. Consequently they were often told to keep quiet and not speak their 'doom and gloom'.[3]

On the other hand, false prophets said no harm would come to God's disobedient people (Jer. 5.12f.; 14.13–16; 23.16–22). Their words were worthless because they dressed the wounds of God's people as if they were not serious (Jer. 6.13–15); they did not expose their sin (Lam. 2.14). Instead they 'prophesied' peace where there was no peace.[4]

The Bible therefore teaches that a genuine prophetic ministry will include a good deal of 'doom and gloom', but in the context of a call to repentance and the assurance of forgiveness and restoration. However, it is possible for prophets to be so influenced by the negative that they begin to mainline on it.

The Spiral of Negativism

Conservatives (evangelical, catholic or plain C of E) and people with a prophetic ministry can, if they are not careful, fall into pernicious pessimism – a downward spiral of negativism encouraged by a fellowship of shared gloom. I have fallen into it myself in the past.

There are various contributory factors in this process. First, discouragement can easily set in. 'The Bishops are not listening and they never speak out about the issues.' 'Deviant, even heretical, clergy are not disciplined.' 'The doctrinal slide is continuing.' 'The gay lobby is gradually eroding the church's resistance and the bishops are giving way.' 'The church is facing financial ruin.' Doom, doom, doom.

Now all of those quotations are to some extent overstatements. But they all contain truth and they are typical of how many clergy and laity feel. Given all this, it is easy to see how people can reach a point where they simply cannot see the good any more. If pressed they might acknowledge there is good in the church, but then the black clouds will close again and they will resume their focus on them.

Second, personality factors are relevant. Some people are naturally rather depressive or pessimistic. Others are naturally argumentative or confrontational. Every Christian ministry is filtered by personality traits, whether strengths or weaknesses. Some people see issues very much in black and white. There are no shades of grey; there is no room for manoeuvre. The situation in the church is either black or white; and since no one believes the church is ever totally pure, these people see it as black.

One of the things which has preserved my sanity (such as it is!) is my highly developed sense of humour. I try to get on with every personality type but I find it extremely difficult to relate to people who lack a sense of humour. When this is the case with conservatives they take themselves and their gloomy feelings far too seriously, and seem unable to see beyond them.

Third, there are social factors. Negativism is contagious. This is where the 'fellowship of shared gloom' comes in. I have often experienced it in the past – conversations which an observer might have thought were contributions to a 'gloomier than thou' contest! The content would be in the category of the quotations I included under the first point above on discouragement; and it is made worse by the fact that like-minded people tend to mix together rather than to dialogue with those who take a different view. So the gloomier souls confirm one another, rather than meeting with their 'opponents' and finding that all is not lost, and there are positive factors in the situation.

By contrast, I have always enjoyed dialogue with those who disagree with me, so long as they could give a good account of themselves. There is nothing I enjoy more than debating with someone who can give me a run for money theologically, and raise points I have not thought of or cannot immediately deal with. Even in my most negative phase this was true, and it was one of the things that saved me from hitting the rock bottom of negativism.

An example of someone whom I believe was caught in a downward spiral is an ex-incumbent I know and respect who published a leaflet giving his *Reasons for Leaving the Church of England* in 1994.[5] I sympathize with some of the points he makes but feel that he then makes statements which are overly negative.

He starts by saying that the church 'officially tolerates error' and instances *The Nature of Christian Belief* which legitimized David Jenkins' denials of credal doctrine and *Issues in Human Sexuality* which 'left room for homosexual practices, at least among lay people'. I have no problem with his view here.

Second, he states the church 'refuses to exercise scriptural discipline. The bishops have refused to declare their policy with regard to practising homosexual clergy. Heretics are not disciplined.' I have some sympathy with this view too, but it is untrue to say that no bishop disciplines practising homosexual clergy. Most of such pastoral work is carried out privately. And it is untrue that no heretical clergy are disciplined. For example, Anthony Freeman, the *Sea of Faith* clergyman, was disciplined by the Bishop of Chichester.

Next he declares that the church 'has rejected the biblical gospel. Justification by Faith is not preached from most Anglican pulpits. The movements that destroy the gospel are allowed to remain – Anglo-Catholicism and Liberalism.' It is here that I begin to part company with the writer. It seems scandalous to me to say the church 'has rejected the biblical gospel'. And how does he know that 'Justification by Faith is not preached from most Anglican pulpits'? I know it is from evangelical pulpits and also know many in the Anglo-Catholic tradition and some in the liberal tradition who most certainly proclaim and live the gospel. Like evangelicalism, both of those traditions contain a spectrum of views. For example, there are liberal liberals and illiberal liberals (or, as I prefer, liberal fundamentalists!).

Fourth, he writes that the church 'denies Christ as the only Saviour and the only way to God' and refers to multifaith services. This simply is not true. *The Bishops' Guidelines on Multifaith Worship* state: 'It is neither appropriate nor lawful for words and actions which are contrary to the Christian Faith to be performed in an Anglican Church' (Para. 130). 'In their participation in such services, Christians should avoid giving the impression that Jesus Christ is merely one of many saviours.'[6]

I respect the writer's courage and personal integrity. But I believe he was to some extent a victim of the downward spiral of negativism.

I myself once wrote to the House of Bishops saying that, because they had effectively legitimized heresy in *The Nature of Christian Belief*, they had committed apostasy. Admittedly, I meant it in the *Oxford English Dictionary* sense of 'unfaithful to religious principles or creed . . . deserting principles or party'[7] (a sense which the New Testament supports)[8] not in the sense of total abandonment of the Faith (which would be a ludicrous criticism in this context). But I withdrew the term because, understandably, some people interpreted it as total abandonment of Christianity. I still believe, though, that however unintentionally on the part of some, and whatever good content the report contained, *The Nature of Christian Belief* effectively legitimized heresy; and this is extremely serious. Nevertheless, I regard my use of that ambiguous term in those circumstances in 1994 as the most serious indication of what I might call my negativist phase in the early 1990s.

It is even possible to reach a point not only of ignoring what is good in the situation but also of virtually delighting in evil, both of which are condemned by St Paul. Every negative news item can seem to be another confirmation of the negativist's position and, if one is brutally frank, can almost be welcomed.

The Curse of Judgementalism

Paul writes that love always protects, always trusts, always hopes, always perseveres' (1 Cor. 13.7) and the context shows the whole verse is referring to our attitude to people. In other words we must avoid cynical distrust of people and never finally give them up as a dead loss.

Contrary to what many of my correspondents believe, the New Testament does tell us to judge. Paul tells the Corinthians that they are to judge those inside the church (1 Cor. 5.12f.).

However the New Testament tells us not to be judgemental, although, on each occasion, in the context we are told to judge. So Jesus says, 'Do not judge, or you too will be judged' (Matt. 7.1) But he goes on to say we should 'remove the speck' from our brother's eye (having removed the plank from our own) and not throw pearls before pigs, both of which require judgement (Matt. 7.5f.).

Paul writes to the Romans: 'Who are you to judge someone else's servant? To his own master he stands or falls . . . You, then, why do you judge your brother? Or why do you look down on your brother? For we will all stand before God's judgement seat. . . . Therefore let us stop passing judgement on one another. Instead, make up your mind not to put any stumbling-block or obstacle in your brother's way' (Rom. 14.4, 10, 13). But he goes on to say in the next chapter: 'I urge you, brothers, to watch out for those who cause divisions and put obstacles in your way that are contrary to the teaching you have learned. Keep away from them' (Rom. 16.17).

James writes that Christians are not to judge their neighbour (Jas. 4.12). But in the next chapter he encourages them to correct those in error, which involves proper judgement (Jas. 5.19f.).

So proper judgement based on biblical principles, prayer and careful analysis is a perfectly proper Christian activity. But judgementalism is not.

Unfortunately there is a fine line between a proper prophetic judgement and such judgementalism. I feel that the leaflet I have just referred to contains elements of judgementalism.

I always tried to do proper research on the evils I was confronting in the church. I felt that the interests of truth, justice and love demanded this of me. And the fact that I not infrequently came across some of the most appalling and ridiculous allegations against Christian leaders, based on prejudice and hearsay, strengthened my resolve in this area. Nevertheless, with hindsight, I recognize that I did begin to fall into judgementalism. I began to question the motives of many bishops and to give up on them.

This contrasts with the attitude of the biblical prophets. It is true that they rebuked kings. Samuel rebuked Saul and announced the Lord's rejection of him, but he still agreed to Saul's request to go back with him to honour him before the elders of Israel. Nathan rebuked David but he also showed him great respect and loyalty.[9]

One of the problems is the accumulated hurts that can occur in the life of someone who tries to carry on an outspoken prophetic ministry. In my case I was prepared for opposition from the liberal establishment but taken aback initially by opposition from evangelicals who did not understand the prophetic ministry. After that I naively thought that my charismatic friends would understand, only to find that many of them understood little about prophecy unless it involved gentle words of encouragement. Although ABWON attracted the support of hundreds of clergy and many more lay people, yet the accumulation of opposition at times seemed to blot out the support. I also noticed that, whereas many Christian leaders in other ministries assured me of their admiration and prayerful support, they did not seem overkeen to invite me onto their platforms! These hurts inevitably strengthen the temptation to judgementalism.

I got to the point in the early 1990s where I really hated going to General Synod. I enjoyed personal contact with people and some good debates, but I hated being so unpopular. Yet I felt obliged to continue fulfilling my prophetic role.

The first Evangelical Anglican Leaders Conference at Westminster Chapel in January 1995 will always stay in my memory as perhaps the lowest point of my sense of hurt at the rejection and opposition engendered by my attempts to be prophetic. I wrote at the time:

> [Having] made some good points and pleaded for unity [the episcopal chairman] began to criticize those of us who feel a biblical obligation publicly to oppose public denials of fundamental doctrine and morality. Throughout the conference, with monotonous regularity, we were got at from the platform. No names were mentioned. But some comments were so tailor-made that I ducked as they came over low in my direction! We were being publicly criticized for making public criticism![10]

Although these comments were accurate I was unaware that God was about to show me that the deep sense of hurt was partly caused by weaknesses which had entered my prophetic ministry in the 1990s. With the benefit of hindsight, I can see that I was beginning to have a vague awareness that something was wrong. But I could not put my finger on it.

Only five months later the light dawned. A minister friend had prayed for my wife and myself during a day conference in

Slough. It was a pleasant experience but did not seem particularly significant. We drove off to Windsor Great Park and walked in the sunshine. Suddenly it was as if a huge weight had lifted from our shoulders and, more important, a veil had fallen from our eyes. We suddenly saw how negative, judgemental and legalistic we had become over the previous four or five years.

I knew that our main ABWON campaigns had been right and stand by them to this day. But ironically at the General Synod at York University, just a few days after the conference, I came to a deeper repentance for the wrong attitudes of negativism, judgementalism and legalism which had crept in during the 1990s. At the same time I began to be overwhelmed with the immensity of God's mercy.

The Paradox of Scripture

The biblical phrase: 'Mercy triumphs over judgement' (Jas. 2.13) kept running through my mind. I came to a new realization that God delights to show mercy; he is rich in mercy.

I immediately launched into a major study of mercy in Scripture. I had read the relevant passages before but now they all but leapt off the page at me. God's mercy is shown even to persistently rebellious sinners. His mercy is exercised after judgement and tempers wrath.[11]

Consequently, showing mercy is an obligation for believers. Jesus said, 'Blessed are the merciful, for they will be shown mercy' (Matt. 5.7). We are to be merciful because God is (Luke 6.36). God 'desires mercy not sacrifice' (Hos. 6.6). 'The wisdom that comes from heaven is . . . full of mercy' (Jas. 3.17).

However, alongside the exciting and liberating rediscovery of mercy came a deep concern. I knew that both church history and experience prove that Christians tend to polarize and become unbalanced. When a 'new' truth is discovered there is a particular danger of reaction. Was I falling into this and veering from a rather negative and judgemental position to one which so focused on mercy it forgot judgement?

How, I asked myself, does one relate all this rich teaching on mercy with the neglected and rather 'heavy' passages I had wrestled with over the years about church discipline, excluding false teachers, the judgement and wrath of God?

A satisfactory answer did not come immediately. Then I reread Revelation 2–3 and I understood the paradox. Why had I not realized it before? This was it – Jesus' prophetic ministry to the churches.

Jesus shows the true 'spirit of prophecy' (Rev. 19.10) in his prophetic messages to the churches in Revelation 2–3. He makes it quite clear that he loves those he rebukes (Rev. 3.19) *and he affirms their good deeds* (except for Laodicea). Here is the paradox – he judges them by very high standards, and with severity, but he also affirms their good deeds.

The Ephesian church had forsaken its first love (for Christ and for each other). However he commended them for their hard work, perseverance and intolerance of wicked men and false teachers, but warned that if they did not repent he would come and remove their lampstand from its place. This means judgement and removal of their witness.

The church in Pergamum was tolerating the presence of false teachers who were commending idolatry and sexual immorality. The latter, particularly, has a remarkably contemporary ring about it. However he commended their faithfulness under persecution, but warned that if they did not repent he would fight against them with the sword of his mouth (the sword of judgement).

Similarly, the church in Thyatira was tolerating a 'prophetess' who was encouraging idolatry and sexual immorality. Nevertheless Jesus commended them for their deeds, love, faith and ever-increasing service but says he will strike down those who follow her.

Jesus shows patience and mercy in giving time for each church to reach repentance.[12] He also promises rich rewards to those who repent after his rebuke.[13]

So a true prophetic ministry will affirm what is good and temper judgement with mercy even with respect to persistently rebellious sinners. It will show patience in giving time for repentance, pointing out God's rich rewards to those who repent. But it will also judge by high standards and point out the severe consequences of impenitence.

However, the mistakes of the Doom and Gloom Brigade are not the only dangers facing those with a prophetic ministry. There are other pitfalls, which we examine in the next chapter.

7 *PITFALLS – THE FLIGHT OF THE FOO-FOO BIRD*

I first heard of the Foo-Foo Bird when I was a teenager at school. It is a mythical bird which flies around in ever-decreasing circles until it finally flies up its own backside! And as I survey the prophetic/conservative scene I think our little feathered friend illustrates a danger facing some Christians. A proper reaction against serious error and yearning for a pure church can, if we are not careful, cause a retreat into the Foo-Foo Syndrome.

The rather depressed Elijah once made this mistake when, as the AV beautifully puts it, he said to the Lord, 'I, even I only, am left, and they seek my life' (1 Kings 19.10). He had been 'very zealous for the Lord' in the face of Israel rejecting the Lord's covenant, breaking down his altars and killing the prophets. The Lord had to tell him: 'I reserve seven thousand in Israel – all whose knees have not bowed down to Baal and all whose mouths have not kissed him' (1 Kings 19.18).

A Place for Separation

There is an opposite danger to the Foo-Foo Syndrome. It has often been said, 'If you find the perfect church don't join it, you'll ruin it.' There is a good deal of truth in that but some Christians so oppose the idea of searching for the pure church that they forget the church is meant to be pure. In fact we are all supposed to be working to make it more pure. Calling for this to happen is at the heart of a true prophetic ministry.

God chose us in Christ 'before the creation of the world to be holy and blameless in his sight' (Eph. 1.4). 'Christ loved the church and gave himself up for her to make her holy, cleansing her by the washing with water through the word, and to present her to himself as a radiant church, without stain or wrinkle or any other blemish, but holy and blameless' (Eph. 5.25–27).

Paul worked hard to present the church as a 'pure virgin' to Christ (Eph. 1.4). He preached, admonished and taught wisely so that he 'may present everyone perfect in Christ' (Col. 1.28).

So we are to 'make every effort to be found spotless, blameless and at peace with him' (2 Pet. 3.14). To do otherwise would be to treat the cross lightly. Christ died for our sins – he died to make the church pure and holy.

Because of all this the New Testament does call us to be separate from doctrinal and moral error. Paul urges Christians to keep away from 'those who cause divisions and put obstacles in your way that are contrary to the teaching you have learned'.[1] Similarly they are not to associate with a Christian who is 'sexually immoral or greedy, an idolater or a slanderer, a drunkard or a swindler' (1 Cor. 5.9–11). The purpose of this is to make the sinner feel ashamed and come to repentance (2 Thess. 3.14). Christians are to 'have nothing to do with the fruitless deeds of darkness, but rather expose them' (Eph. 5.11).

John urges Christians not to give hospitality to false teachers (the context is denial of the incarnation) because to do so would be to share their wicked work.[2]

This teaching must be taken seriously, and all too often the church does not do so. The Church of England is weak on godly discipline (and, to be fair, so are other denominations). It would be interesting to ask whether some of those who speak out so strongly against false teaching and the toleration of immorality within the national church actually practise loving, godly, biblical discipline in their own local church. It is easy to call for the bishops to discipline 'them out there', but it is one of the most difficult and painful things to practise proper discipline in one's own congregation.

As we have seen Jesus gives the steps of loving correction which are at the heart of godly discipline within the church:

> If your brother sins against you, go and show him his

> fault, just between the two of you. If he listens to you, you have won your brother over. But if he will not listen, take one or two others along, so that 'every matter may be established by the testimony of two or three witnesses.' If he refuses to listen to them, tell it to the church; and if he refuses to listen even to the church, treat him as you would a pagan or a tax collector.[3]

So a person in serious error (e.g. persistent immorality or divisive rebellion) should be approached privately and gently (Gal. 6.1). If that does not bring necessary repentance, objective witnesses should be involved to assess the situation and, if necessary, urge repentance. If that is not successful the church should be asked to urge the person to repent. And finally, if still impenitent, the person should be regarded as out of fellowship. However, throughout this whole process the motive and intention should be to restore the person in error.

That is hard teaching for our easy-going, relativistic culture. But it is the teaching of Jesus, so Christians can hardly be justified in ignoring it. Nevertheless we should apply it with sensitivity, e.g. by 'tell the church' I have in serious cases given a brief explanation in a confidential meeting of certain church leaders and members, on a 'need to know' basis.

The Perils of Separation

However, the teaching on separation from unbiblical doctrine and behaviour needs to be properly understood in context. First, none of these passages speak of seceding from the local church. They usually deal with procedure in the case of an individual who has offended the local church. Or they tackle the matter of separating from false apostles. One assumes that a false apostle would be asked to leave and a true apostle invited to replace him. There were no denominations in those days. There was probably only one church to go to in any one place. To leave that one local church was to leave the church entirely. I am not saying that secession has never been right or necessary throughout history. But I am saying that the New Testament teaching is about putting an individual out of fellowship (in extreme cases) or refusing to accept the authority of some teachers, etc. within or over a congregation.

Although these passages speak of not welcoming false teachers, or disciplining those involved in immorality, heresy or divisiveness, the New Testament is silent as to what a believer should do if the leadership of a congregation became totally apostate and refused to repent or leave.

Second, unity is a very high priority in Scripture. It is the very purpose of God to bring the church to unity. It is his gift to the church, and the effect of Pentecost.[4] In the traumatic circumstances of the night he was betrayed, Jesus prayed earnestly that the church would be as completely united as he is with the Father (John 17.11, 22f.). Unity is the very essence of the church. It is one body and each member belongs to all the others (Rom. 12.5; 1 Cor. 12.12). The members should have equal concern for one another and share each other's suffering and joy (1 Cor. 12.25–27). Paul urged the Corinthians: 'all of you agree with one another so that there may be no divisions among you and that you may be perfectly united in mind and thought' (1 Cor. 1.10). He taught that unity is essential in the battle against evil (Phil. 1.27–30).

So we are to 'make every effort to keep the unity of the Spirit through the bond of peace' (Eph. 4.3). Following the example of Christ, we are to be 'like-minded, having the same love, being one in spirit and purpose'; to 'do nothing out of selfish ambition or vain conceit, but in humility consider others better than' ourselves. We should look not only to our own interests, but also to the interests of others (Phil. 2.1–5). We should practise compassion, kindness, humility, gentleness and patience, bearing with and forgiving one another, and over all these virtues putting on love, 'which binds them all together in perfect unity' (Col. 3.12–14).

It is therefore an extremely serious matter to divide the church of God. I think that some prophetic people and conservatives do not realize just how serious. We must separate from serious and persistent evil, but dividing the church is also a serious evil.

Third, we really must distinguish between primary and secondary matters. The New Testament calls us to have nothing to do with persistent *primary* error in doctrine or behaviour. But not infrequently Christians separate over secondary issues (often matters which have no doctrinal or ethical significance whatsoever!). This is wrong. I normally live dangerously, so for what it is worth, I will give my list of primary and secondary issues. I do not claim it is divinely inspired and binding on every Christian! But it is my position.

The primary purpose of Scripture is to make clear the way of salvation, therefore I believe primary beliefs are those vital to the doctrine of salvation – they are gospel issues. Gospel issues include: credal beliefs (covering the nature of God, the person and work of Christ, etc.); the normative divine inspiration of Scripture without which we would not know of salvation; the explicit moral law taught in Scripture (Jesus upheld the Ten Commandments and their implications. The Pauline epistles and others specify sins which will, if persisted in, prevent a person entering the kingdom). I would also include clear issues of justice.

I define a secondary issue as one which does not fit into the category above and on which numerous Christians, with an equally high view of Scripture, interpret the Bible differently, giving full weight to the traditional interpretation and using sound hermeneutical (interpretative) principles. I believe it is sinful to divide the church, or divide from the church, over secondary issues.

We need to be objective about secondary issues. Any of us can subjectively elevate our favourite secondary issue into a primary issue or a shibboleth by which we judge other people's orthodoxy. So I would include under secondary issues: the *method* of divine inspiration of Scripture and its detailed implications; the *method* by which God created the universe; particular understandings of the baptism of the Spirit as opposed to teaching about being filled with the Spirit; particular emphases about the gifts of the Holy Spirit including tongues and prophecy; different views of healing; particular understandings of revival and movements of the Holy Spirit; differences as to the mode and timing of baptism; differences between a view of holy communion as an aid to focusing on Christ and a view of it as spiritually, by faith, feeding on Christ; confirmation; differences over forms of church government, ordination and order.

I would also include differences over the place of women's ministry (it is recognized that some regard male headship as a primary issue, but I do not believe it is a gospel issue); patterns of worship – liturgical and 'non-liturgical', traditional and modern, restrained and extrovert; differences over demonology, spiritual warfare; deliverance, counselling; responsible differences over drawing the line between acceptable behaviour and sinful compromise regarding New Age involvement, where Scripture is not explicit, e.g. alternative therapies; views of ethics in areas where Scripture is not explicit, e.g. some views of remarriage; (non-abortive) family planning; pacifism; capital punishment; political views; cultural differences including differences over music and the arts; details of eschatology: millennial views; views of the rapture, the tribulation and Israel. There must be many others which I have not mentioned.

It is important to note that secondary issues may have parameters (limits) beyond which a primary issue is raised. For example, the issue of whether the second coming is before or after the millennium is a secondary issue, but the literal second coming of Jesus is a primary issue.

Jesus himself upset the religious establishment by not following the traditions which had gained respect over the years. He did not keep all the fasts or the current observance of the Sabbath or the ritual ablutions or the ceremonial separation from 'unclean' Samaritans (even an immoral Samaritan woman).

Paul regards differences over food and drink and holy days as secondary issues (Rom. 14.1–6). Yet Christians have at times divided over food and especially drink; and they have at times divided over how Sunday should be observed.

We have seen that secession is not mentioned in the New

Testament. It advocates dealing with primary error in doctrine and behaviour *within* the church by discipline, or refusing to welcome false teachers from elsewhere. It also teaches the vital importance of maintaining unity. Another consideration is that the subsequent history of secession in the church (however justified) is not a happy one. Division tends to breed division.

Early Methodism illustrates the point. John Wesley never intended to secede from the Church of England (however much his actions and opposition to him precipitated secession). He died in 1791. In 1797 the Methodist New Connexion seceded from the Methodist Conference. In 1805 the Independent Methodists also seceded followed by the Primitive Methodists in 1810 and the Bible Christians in 1815. The departure of the Wesleyan Methodist Association occurred in 1835; and the Wesleyan Reformers seceded in 1849. However those two bodies united to form the United Methodist Free Churches in 1857. In the twentieth century other groups reunited.

Even the new churches, which used to be called house-churches, have divided into various streams over the last couple of decades, although more recently there tends to be more fellowship between them.

The Free Church of England began informally in Devon in 1844 after, it is alleged, the Bishop of Exeter withdrew the licence of a clergyman simply because he was an evangelical. It acquired legal status in 1863. It continues to this day but acknowledges it is 'still a tiny denomination'.[5]

It is interesting that *some* of the smaller denominations seem to make little impact and some of the larger denominations seem no better than the older churches like the Church of England. What is more, God does not seem to have seceded from the older churches – there is still much blessing evident in them.

After stressing unity, it is important for me to say that I do not comment on these other denominations and streams negatively. They are brothers and sisters in Christ and I have friends in all of them.

However, history affords evidence of the Foo-Foo Syndrome.

Once a Christian starts the process of separation, unless he heeds the warnings I have outlined in this chapter, he can easily fall into it. First, he (rightly) separates from some Christians who persist in primary error, say, who deny the virgin birth or bodily resurrection of Christ, who allow multifaith worship in a Christian context, even marginalize or exclude Jesus, or promote homosexual practice. He finds fellowship in the grouping that shares his views on those errors.

Then he begins to find what he perceives as errors in this group. One of them believes in infant baptism. Another affirms the charismatic definition of baptism in the Spirit. A third believes women are allowed to preach. This is too much, so he separates from this group.

He is not alone, others feel the same way and join him in this second group. All is fine to begin with until he discovers that one of them does not believe in the secret pre-millennial rapture of the church. Another does not hold to the prophetic significance of modern Israel. A third does not believe in creation in a literal six days. This really is intolerable, so he separates from this group.

And so it goes on until he reaches a point where he says to his long-suffering wife (to misquote the old saying): 'All the church is bad, save me and thee, and even thee's a bit off.' Or, shades of Elijah, 'I, even I only am left, and they seek my life.'

I receive a magazine from a sincere Christian involved in prophetic ministry. I respect his integrity but am worried by what I read. Referring to churches of all denominations he speaks of: 'The imperative to come out . . . the parting of the ways.' Speaking of Christians leaving 'unsuitable churches', he comments: 'This was the Lord's plan. When the Israelites turned to idols in the desert, 'the Lord spake unto Moses and Aaron, saying, "Separate yourselves from among this congregation, that I may consume them in a moment"' (Num. 16.20–21).

'What does this scattering mean, then?' he asks, 'I believe that we are experiencing a transition from the visible denominational "churches" of today back to the original Church of the Body of Christ.'[6]

Later he quotes, with approval, someone who wrote: 'It is possible that the age of the church in terms of [local assemblies of believers] may already be over or ending.' He explains that he has not attended *any* church consistently for years, explaining: 'I simply cannot assemble together with those who unrepentantly and repeatedly teach obvious demonstrable error. I tried but can't do it. I continue to assemble with other believers, privately and individually, but not under [local assemblies of believers]. In that sense for me, for now, the age of the church is over.'[7]

This is not a tenable position in New Testament terms but it graphically illustrates the danger, which people have fallen into time and again in church history. Some Anglicans, as well as people of other denominations, are being beguiled by this extreme pure church quest. *Much as I respect their integrity, I believe them to be deceived by a subtle divide-and-conquer strategy. The devil has been in the business long enough to deceive even those who for conscientious or prophetic reasons are earnestly seeking purity in the church.*

However, a wrong approach to the biblical teaching on separation and error is not the only danger facing conservative and prophetic people.

The Pitfall of Legalism

One of the main dangers facing conservative Christian circles (evangelical, Catholic or plain traditional) is legalism. A very high view of Scripture can lead Christians to regard it as a legal code rather than revealing the living word of God.

The word of God, expressed in Scripture and ultimately in Christ, 'is eternal; it stands firm in the heavens' (Ps. 119.89). It revives the soul; gives joy to the heart and light to the eyes. It is more precious than gold and sweeter than the honeycomb (Ps. 19.7–10). It inspires endurance and gives encouragement, comfort, guidance, eternal life and hope. It also convicts of sin and can prevent us sinning.[8]

Little wonder then that the psalmist loves God's word, rejoices and delights in it and sings of it.[9] What a contrast this is to legalism!

One of the mistakes that leads conservatives and prophetic people into legalism is an unbalanced approach to God's word. We have seen that a significant amount of a prophetic ministry will be warning of judgement. But we saw too that Jesus, the great prophet to the New Testament churches, also stressed the strengths and good points of the churches he was warning of judgement.

For some ten years of my public prophetic ministry I did not get this balance right. Having scrutinized them carefully in the light of what I subsequently learned, I still stand by the campaigns and the main criticisms I made in those years. And it would not be true to say that I never spoke of the good points of the Church of England – I did fairly frequently. But, had I achieved a more Christ-like balance, it would have been an obvious note of my ministry – commendation as well as critical warning.

But I was so taken with the importance of biblical teaching on the virgin birth and bodily resurrection of Christ; his uniqueness as the only Saviour; the sinfulness of homosexual practice and the judgement that Scripture showed would come upon a church tolerating the denial of those truths, that I seriously neglected its teaching on affirmation and mercy.

The imbalance must have given an unintentional legalistic impression. I have already said that I should not have allowed myself to be dragged into the quota-capping debate. I remember giving a paper at a well-attended day conference in London organized by Reform. In my talk I held forth with great conviction on the logic of quota-capping for theological reasons.

I stated it is right to give to individuals in personal need irrespective of their views on the faith. Even needy enemies are to be helped. But, I said, the situation is different with churches which are unbiblical in belief or behaviour and added various reasons why financial support should not be given to seriously failing churches. First, I argued that we must be apostolic in strongly opposing false teaching. I pointed out that the

Judaizers amongst the Galatians were anathematized by Paul. They were undermining the gospel with legalism.

I added that those denying the incarnation were antichrists and liars. Anyone who welcomes them shares in their wicked work. Is denying the virgin birth with the resultant adoptionist implications any better? Also the Durham Controversy included statements that Christians did not need to believe in the incarnation.

Second, I argued that we must separate from wrong behaviour. *Persistently* immoral church people must be put out of fellowship; we must not associate with them. Their evil 'yeast' will spread in the church. Similarly we must be separate from the *persistently* greedy, idolaters, slanderers, drunkards and swindlers and we must separate from those who are persistently idle or refuse apostolic teaching.

Third, I stated we must be Christ-like towards compromising, apathetic churches. Ironically I referred to Revelation 2–3 (the very passage God later used to show the imbalance in my ministry) and said the attitude of Jesus to the churches in Asia Minor contrasts with the outlook of the modern church. He warns even good churches, whose strengths he commends, that he will judge them if they persist in certain weaknesses.

So, I argued, Jesus judges even otherwise good churches which have lost their first love or compromise with the world or tolerate immorality or are spiritually lukewarm. Should statements that the Church of England is under God's judgement therefore be a surprise? I concluded:

> It is plain from the New Testament that we are not to support churches which persist in being *clearly* unbiblical in belief or behaviour. But it is equally wrong to support churches which persist in being apathetic and that must include churches who are not bothering to give sacrificially – which is most Anglican churches. Weak giving is clearly unbiblical.

I remember a theologian friend saying to me after the talk: 'Yes, you are right, it is absolutely clear from Scripture. There is no doubt about it.' And there wasn't – until the Lord opened my eyes to his mercy. Obviously, I still hold we must be apostolic in strongly opposing clearly unbiblical teaching and behaviour. And I still believe quota-capping (after paying one's way to the diocese) is justified in extreme circumstances where there is persistence in primary error in doctrine or behaviour. But I now see Jesus' attitude towards apathetic churches differently. I see God as a God of overwhelming mercy.

The Priority of Mercy

As already noted, I have been quite overwhelmed by the way God shows his mercy to persistently rebellious sinners. I began to do a major biblical study on it. I noted that Nehemiah writes:

> Our forefathers, became arrogant and stiff-necked, and did not obey your commands. . . . They killed your prophets . . . So you handed them over to their enemies, who oppressed them. . . . And when they cried out to you again, you heard from heaven, and in your compassion you delivered them time after time. . . . But in your great mercy you did not put an end to them or abandon them, for you are a gracious and merciful God.[10]

Daniel affirms: 'The Lord our God is merciful and forgiving, even though we have rebelled against him' (Dan. 9.9). Paul writes: 'For God has bound all men over to disobedience so that he may have mercy on them all' (Rom. 11.32). And he adds his testimony: 'Even though I was once a blasphemer and a persecutor and a violent man, I was shown mercy because I acted in ignorance and unbelief' (1 Tim. 1.13).

Then I remembered a book I had bought at college by Professor Norman Snaith. In an exhaustive study of the Hebrew word *chesed*, often translated *mercy*, he says: 'The word means "faithfulness" rather than "kindness", for we find the word to involve, in almost every case, a substratum of fixed, determined, almost stubborn steadfastness. . . . The best word is "covenant-love".'[11]

He continues, 'The most important of all the distinctive ideas of the Old Testament is God's steady and extraordinary persistence in continuing to love wayward Israel in spite of Israel's insistent waywardness.'[12]

Finally he refers to the dilemma of the prophets.

> What is the balance of Mercy and Justice? The prophets solved it, as Rashi . . . said, by giving 'precedence to the rule of mercy' and joining 'it with the rule of justice' . . . [God's] demand for Right Action is so insistent that it could not be more so, but his chesed for the people of his choice is more insistent still. This may seem contradictory, but it is true. God's determination is that the bond between him and Israel shall never ultimately be broken, that the covenant shall survive, even though with the smallest remnant.
>
> . . . God cares more for mercy than he cares for righteousness . . . but not because he cares one whit less than maximum for righteousness. If God's mercy is to be greater than his demand for righteousness, then how wondrous great his mercy must be, and how steadfast and insistent. We do not make his demand for righteousness any the less. Rather we demonstrate the surpassing wonder of his unfailing covenant-love.[13]

Snaith expresses very well the supremacy of mercy and yet the absolute demand of righteousness. The emphasis of the Old Testament prophets was on the corporate people of God rather than the individual. But it is clear that, because we are referring to the nature of God, he would show the same attitude to individuals. It does not, of course, mean that judgement will never be meted out on individuals or churches. But it does illustrate God's abundant mercy towards sinful, rebellious, and even apostate, human beings. God is no legalist. Nor should we be.

In my own study of Scripture I noted how God used Old

Testament people of faith (Heb. 11) in spite of their failings.

I also noted that God took Israel back to the land from exile before they repented, even though he said they must repent before he would do so. The Lord is so merciful that although he lays down repentance as the condition of restoration, he does not seem to keep strictly to this. The Israelites had already returned to the land before Ezra led them in repentance (Neh. 9). It is true that there was a good deal of fasting during the exile but the Lord said that much of the fasting of the exiles was insincere (Zech. 7.4–7).

The first group returned from exile in 538 BC. But in 520 Zechariah is still calling them to return to the Lord (Zech. 1.1–6). In the same year Haggai accuses them of selfishly neglecting to build the temple (Hag. 1.1–11). The Lord said through him that whatever the nation did and offered was defiled (Hag. 2.14). In 458 BC Ezra discovered to his horror that the returned exiles had intermarried with pagan wives, a practice which would almost inevitably lead them into idolatry. Yet idolatry was the main cause of the exile. Ezra leads them in public repentance (Ezra 9–10). In 446 BC Nehemiah confessed that the people had '*acted very wickedly towards*' God. He included himself and his house.

The following year Ezra publicly read the Book of the Law to the people, who were clearly ignorant of it. They wept at its contents (Neh. 8). Ezra led them in public repentance acknowledging that the exile and their present state were a just judgement by God. The people then covenanted to obey God. This major repentance, reading of the neglected law, and covenant to obey God's law took place *ninety-three* years after the first exiles were restored to the land. Even so Malachi, after this (probably after 433 BC), prophesied against the sins of the people which included offering blemished sacrifices, intermarriage with pagans, sorcery, adultery, perjury, social oppression and withholding tithes from the Lord. The Lord pronounces a curse on the priests who have dishonoured him and led the people astray.[14]

All of this supports the contention that God in his mercy

restored the exiles to the land before there was real, widespread repentance, and even after that, there were times of regression.

I also took note of how God used the disciples in spite of their failings. They had little faith, even after the resurrection, and misunderstood his mission. They were place-seeking. They failed to support Jesus in his passion and deserted him when he was arrested. Peter denied Christ. Yet they were used in preaching, healing and exorcisms during Jesus' ministry, and were greatly used after Pentecost despite further failings (e.g. the dispute between Paul and Barnabas).

Similarly God used the New Testament churches in spite of their failings. They suffered from racial selfishness, unbelieving prayer, legalism, sharp disputes, quarrels, anger, slander, gossip, divisions and factions. There was judgementalism, jealousy, arrogance and boasting, toleration of immorality, selfishness even at holy communion and materialism. Some were extreme charismatics, antinomians or false teachers. Others suffered from idleness because of their extreme eschatological views.[15]

Take, for instance, the Corinthian church. Its sins included incest; justification of other sexual immorality; drunkenness at communion; 'charismatic chaos'; disorderly behaviour by women; denial of the resurrection of the body.

Paul condemned this behaviour and urged believers to avoid and expel those who persisted in it. But God still used this church. For example, he gave genuine gifts of the Spirit to the Corinthian church. However the first chapters of Revelation do point out that a time of judgement would come if there was no repentance.

As I have studied and thought about the love God has for all his creation and his overwhelming mercy as shown in Scripture, I have developed a much more positive attitude towards people, including non-Christians and Christian leaders in serious error (while maintaining a clear opposition to that error).

My new understanding of the unfathomable riches of God's mercy is overwhelming both to mind and heart. I define it as follows: 'God's mercy may be described as his taking an absolute (perfect) stand on the principles he has revealed in Scripture but nevertheless blessing richly those who disobey those principles (while calling them to repentance)!'

The Problem of Fundamentalism

Another cause of legalism arises from aspects of fundamentalism. Unfortunately there are a number of mutually inconsistent definitions of fundamentalism. So much so that the word is unhelpful except perhaps as a 'put down' for views of which one disapproves. The word 'liberal' can be used in the same unhelpful way, but by different people!

For some, simply regarding the Bible as reliable and authoritative is fundamentalist. For others, standing for the truth of every aspect of the historic creeds is fundamentalist. There are those who regard being an evangelical as fundamentalist.

But a more accurate definition of Christian fundamentalism has recently been given by the Evangelical Alliance. It states that fundamentalists:

1. are suspicious of scholarship and science and tend to be anti-intellectual;
2. have a 'mechanical' view of how the Bible was written;
3. believe the Authorized (King James) Version of the Bible to be the only inspired translation;
4. have a literalistic approach to interpreting the Bible;
5. reject involvement with Christians who do not hold their views;
6. often allow their culture to influence their beliefs – thus some support racial intolerance, 'prosperity teaching' and politically right-wing views;
7. have denied, until recently, that the Christian gospel has social implications;
8. insist on certain views concerning the second coming of Christ.

It is easy to see how legalistic such a fundamentalist approach can be. There is a good deal of fear involved in it – fear of scholarship, fear of liberalism, etc.; and it is a narrow, intolerant, exclusivist position.

I reject all these points. It is my conviction that a prophetic ministry needs to have an open attitude towards a critical academic study of theology. The prophet should consult works by scholars from a wide variety of theological views as well as those of secular authors. This will assist in exploration of theology and of interpretation of the biblical text. A prophet should refuse to follow uncritically a traditional evangelical (or any other traditional) interpretation. It is only such a self-critical approach to theology which will not only avoid legalism, but will enable the prophet to speak and debate with conviction and credibility.

Secondary differences should not prevent our co-operating with as wide a range as possible of Christians (and, where relevant, non-Christians). And we must remember that we are all heavily influenced by culture, but every culture needs to be redeemed by the gospel.

It is all very well doing a critical analysis of the Foo-Foo Syndrome. But some people feel that the Church of England is in such a bad state, in terms of doctrinal and moral confusion, that Christians who have any prophetic insight should withdraw from it. I believe they are mistaken.

Why Not Leave the Church of England?

In brief, it is my conviction that we should remain within the Church of England and work constructively, patiently and mercifully for reformation. However, if the national leadership as a body were to embrace heresy, we should regard ourselves as in impaired communion with that leadership, rather than leave. My reasons are as follows.

First, because the Church of England still remains officially committed to the supremacy of Scripture. The Canon Law of the Church clearly states this:

> The doctrine of the Church of England is grounded in the Holy Scriptures, and in such teachings of the ancient

> Fathers and Councils of the Church as are agreeable to the said Scriptures. In particular such doctrine is to be found in the Thirty-nine Articles of Religion, the Book of Common Prayer, and the Ordinal. (Canon A5)
>
> The Thirty-nine Articles are agreeable to the Word of God and may be assented unto with a good conscience by all members of the Church of England. (Canon A2)

The Thirty-nine Articles clearly state:

> Holy Scripture containeth all things necessary to salvation: so that whatsoever is not read therein, nor may be proved thereby, is not to be required of any man, that it should be believed as an article of the Faith, or to be thought requisite or necessary to salvation (Article 6).
>
> The Church hath power to decree Rites or Ceremonies, and authority in Controversies of Faith: And yet it is not lawful for the Church to ordain any thing that is contrary to God's Word written, neither may it so expound one place of Scripture, that it be repugnant to another. Wherefore, although the Church be a witness and a keeper of holy Writ, yet, as it ought not to decree any thing against the same, so besides the same it ought not to enforce any thing to be believed for necessity of salvation. (Article 20)

So, for example, the Articles clearly affirm the virginal conception and bodily resurrection of Christ; Jesus as the only Saviour; justification by grace through faith.[16]

It follows from all this that true Anglicans are those who willingly accept the authority of Holy Scripture, including over the virgin birth and bodily resurrection of Christ who is the only Saviour. That is not to deny the value of tradition and reason (which greatly influence all Christians, whether they realize it or not), but they should not be used in such a way as to undermine Scripture.

Some who have left the Church of England point out that the General Synod can change the doctrinal basis of the church, so its biblical foundation is insecure. It is true that the General Synod has the power to make decisions 'touching the doctrinal formulae . . . of the Church of England'.[17] But clearly these decisions are to be consistent with the Canons and Articles mentioned above (the synod made a total revision of the Canons in the 1960s and from time to time makes minor revisions or additions to them).

Such doctrinal decisions have to be approved by a two-thirds majority in each house of the synod (bishops, clergy, laity). The House of Bishops must previously discuss the matter separately. And the leadership of the two Convocations (clergy elected to the synod from Canterbury and from York Provinces) and of the House of Laity may also decide to have separate debates and make separate decisions on the matter. It is highly unlikely that these Canons and Articles would be significantly changed.

The women priests decision shows that the synod can make important theological decisions based upon a particular (majority) interpretation of Scripture, so long as it does not contradict an explicit doctrinal belief of the church. A legal challenge on the decision failed, showing the synod's power in this respect.

Were the synod to pass a resolution affirming homosexual practice (an unlikely event in the foreseeable future) many of us believe this would contravene Article 20, quoted above, which states 'it is not lawful for the Church to ordain any thing that is contrary to God's Word written, neither may it so expound one place of Scripture, that it be repugnant to another'. As Article 20 would still remain intact, those who uphold it in this matter would be true to the teaching of the Anglican Church, and therefore should remain, while refusing the authority of those who passed the unscriptural resolution.

My second reason for believing it right to stay within the Church of England is the biblical teaching, outlined earlier, that maintaining unity is of vital importance in the church, and this is a prophetic issue. We ought not to divide or separate within the church unless it is over a persistent primary error in doctrine or morality and even then, where possible, we should form a church within a church. I see no such primary error in the *official* teaching of the church. We should not divide the church over secondary issues.

However, those two reasons are based upon the official position of the church. What about the actual situation, the unofficial errors? After all, these are of deep significance to anyone with a prophetic ministry. Even George Carey himself said in 1990, just before becoming archbishop: 'We are under judgement because we have been lukewarm, and that is why some of our keenest people have left us and gone to other churches. We have been disobedient. We have not followed the law of the Lord. We have been sinful and faithless. We have put up with standards in our churches which are a disgrace to the Church of God.'[18]

If the Church of England is under judgement, what are people like me doing staying within it? Reference back to Scripture gives the answer and my third reason for staying within the church.

In the wilderness a whole generation of Israelites were under God's judgement. They would never enter the promised land. Yet Moses was called to continue witnessing prophetically to God's word among them for forty years, even though judgement was inevitable.

Similarly Jesus wept over the inevitable judgement on Jerusalem then, in holy anger, continued to speak and act prophetically. He immediately carried out the prophetic action of cleansing the temple.

According to Scripture, the fact that a people or church are under judgement does not necessarily mean that those who are obedient to God (including those with a prophetic ministry) should withdraw from it. (See above on separating within rather than separating from the church.)

A fourth reason is that God does not appear to have left the Church of England! (I do realize the Lord is not an Anglican!) He is still powerfully blessing and using many good local Anglican churches. This is the real frontier of the church. We should be grateful for it, support it and relate to it. Wherever there is a move of the Holy Spirit one finds many Anglican churches involved. I do not want to sound denominationalist (God only has one church, to which all Christians belong), but there really is no reliable evidence that God is blessing Anglican churches less than those of other denominations, old or new.

My other reasons for staying within the Church of England are secondary, and would not in themselves be sufficient. They are nevertheless important. I value the liturgy of the church and its rich, balanced framework. I also appreciate the psychological and spiritual value of dignified ceremonial.

Another factor is the sense of historical continuity. One value of a strong sense of history and tradition is that it encourages self-criticism in those who, like me, want to be radically biblical and to see the church reformed accordingly. It can correct, purify and ultimately strengthen our understanding of the challenge of biblical radicalism. We can learn from and hopefully avoid the mistakes of the past, when making changes, while holding onto what is good from the past.

The parish concept encourages the local church to be outward-looking, involved in society and evangelistic. Then there is the historical influence of the Church of England upon the nation. It can have influence for good within Parliament and other institutions, the media and the general population.

There is another consideration. The New Testament knows only of the local and universal church, not of denominations. It follows from this that, from the point of view of biblical ecclesiology, a local church is primarily to be judged by its own beliefs and behaviour, not that of its denomination

Nevertheless, this does not lead me to a congregational view of the church which holds each congregation is independent and autonomous. The New Testament clearly teaches that local congregations, as part of the one catholic (universal) church, should network together in mutual responsibility and interdependence, benefiting from trans-local ministries. It is also important for ministers to be examined and validated by the wider church.

Also the biblical ideal is that the local church consists of all the believers in a particular locality – a village, town or city.

However, after 2000 years of denominational traditions we have to accept the reality of denominations, particularly as historically some were formed in an attempt to separate from error over primary issues.

Although a local church should be judged on its own beliefs and behaviour, yet it has responsibilities concerning the denomination to which it belongs. If that denomination falls into serious error the local church, far from ignoring that and so appearing to support it in error, must show disapproval, particularly in the Church of England where ministry is received directly from the bishops in ordination, confirmation, etc. If the error is serious the local church may need to take firm action.

The New Testament does urge separation from trans-local leaders who are in serious error. The apostles strongly opposed the false teaching and practice of so-called apostles, risking division in so doing.

Paul warned the Corinthians about false apostles in the church who rejected his apostolic authority. We may parallel them with modern Christian leaders who reject the authority of apostolic (biblical) teaching. Paul called them servants of Satan (2 Cor. 11.13–15).

He warned the Galatians of false teachers in the church who were undermining the gospel with 'another gospel' of salvation by works. He calls down a curse on them (Gal. 1.8–9). He warns other churches against false teachers and their deceitful scheming (Eph. 4.14) and hollow philosophy (Col. 2.8).

John also calls false teachers in the church who deny the incarnation 'antichrists' (1 John 2.18f.) and he warns of false prophets (1 John 4.1). Peter condemns false teachers who exploit the faithful (2 Pet. 2.3).

It is quite clear that the apostles would use equally strong language and risk division over church leaders who hold or legitimize the holding of the following views: that the virgin birth of Christ is unhistorical; that the bodily resurrection of Christ may not have happened; that Jesus will not return in his risen body to the world; that homosexual or other immoral practice is acceptable in certain circumstances; that it is acceptable for Christians to be involved in multifaith worship which marginalizes or excludes Christ or involves worship of other deities, or gives the impression that all faiths are equal or offer ways of salvation.

According to 2 John 10–11 anyone who welcomes a false teacher 'shares in his wicked work'. Separating from those leaders who are persistently and deliberately heretical over primary issues is a biblical obligation. But, as we have seen, biblical teaching envisages separation within not separation from the church.

We also have a biblical obligation to act mercifully. One of the issues raised by Reform is the appointment of their own bishops, if necessary, because of disillusionment with the present hierarchy. This causes me deep concern because I believe it would be a schismatic action. I am unable to think of a likely scenario where I personally could accept it. It would surely only be if the whole House of Bishops were knowingly and persistently embracing primary false teaching.

I believe the right approach is to take the most conservative action which is consistent with all the relevant biblical teaching. It may well remain the case that most orthodox Anglicans are not in a position of impaired communion with their own bishop.

But when it is proven that a bishop knowingly and persistently affirms primary false teaching (which is the case in certain places) clergy and parishes are obliged to inform him that they require alternative episcopal oversight. They should first ask him to provide it, but if that fails they should then ask the archbishop to provide it, e.g. another bishop – suffragan, assistant or retired – in the diocese, a flying bishop (Provincial Episcopal Visitor, PEV), or a bishop from another diocese.

It is only if all this fails that they should themselves consider approaching another existing bishop, even from the wider Anglican communion, to provide oversight, although this could lead to a legal challenge. Given Christian goodwill on all sides and the establishment of the principle of flying bishops, there should be no need to go as far as this let alone beyond it.

I firmly believe that following the teaching of Scripture would ensure that, as far as Christians are concerned, the Foo-Foo Bird would be extinct.

8 EPILOGUE

It was Ian Hislop, editor of *Private Eye*, who said: 'Is the Church of England in crisis? Well, yes. But then it normally is.' And, he added: 'Its demise is consistently behind schedule.'[1] Despite Hislop being one of my least favourite people, I have to admit that his television documentary on the Church of England, during which he made these remarks, was excellent and this comment is very perceptive, even prophetic!

Prophets need not only a sense of proportion and a sense of humour but also a sense of history. The church has been through great crises before, and suffered immense damage. At times it has seemed that God was largely working outside it, for example in the Pentecostal Revival. But, in fact, sooner or later it appears that the good things happening outside or on the fringe of the Church of England became part of its mainstream. For example, Pentecostalism which was excluded in the early 1900s, now widely affects the Church of England in the charismatic movement. No doubt those in the Catholic tradition would say the same about the Oxford Movement.

Is it therefore safe for the church to ignore the prophetic ministry when it warns of the dangers facing it? Perhaps a salutary lesson can be learnt from the situation currently facing the monarchy. It is quite remarkable how quickly there has been a sea change of attitude towards it. True, TV polls have shown a majority still support it, but their statistical reliability is, to say the least, in doubt. But who would have thought a decade or so ago that we would even be debating its future on television? Many are asking whether the monarchy will survive the death of the Queen, except perhaps in the very reduced state of some mainland European monarchies.

Is the Church of England so secure that it will always, as in history, ride the storms of controversy, numerical decline and spiritual degeneration? It would be foolish to rely on such an opinion.

Personal Accountability

In any case, whatever the future holds for a church or a denomination each Christian is answerable personally to God. Those of us in leadership, especially ordained leadership, 'must give account' to God for how we have fulfilled it (Heb. 13.17). On the Day of Judgement 'the fire will test the quality of each man's work'. What is merely 'wood, hay or straw' will be burnt up (1 Cor. 3.10–15). Little wonder James warns: 'Not many of you should presume to become teachers, my brothers, because you know that we who teach will be judged more strictly' (Jas. 3.1). It is therefore no use those who ignored the destructive 'liberalism' of the 1980s consoling themselves that in the 1990s the Church of England is to some extent in a better state. They will be answerable for what they did in their generation. And I strongly recommend repentance to them and to those responsible for that liberalism.

What else do I believe God is currently saying to the Church of England?

Recent Improvements

I believe the situation from the mid-1990s has been far more encouraging than in the fifteen years before that. The House of Bishops is more orthodox with fewer exceptions. I have written to them twice recently, once about my paradigm shift over mercy and secondly about the Southwark Cathedral service for the Lesbian and Gay Christian Movement. The replies were most encouraging, but see below. The Archbishop of Canterbury speaks out for orthodox beliefs and traditional family values, as well as social issues. At first he appeared to be compromising on the uniqueness of Christ as the only Saviour in some of his pronouncements and when he vehemently opposed the

Open Letter on the subject. But there have been virtually no multifaith services in Church of England buildings since the Open Letter. What about the other main issues?

Doctrinal Views

There have been controversies over episcopal belief in the past. But there was always a public display of requiring such bishops to affirm orthodox belief. The sinister new factor about the way the House of Bishops responded to the Durham Controversy was that they legitimized what was traditionally regarded as heresy. For the first time ever the House of Bishops of the Church of England, in effect, justified heresy. They did not adopt the heresy, but they allowed it as an acceptable option for bishops. That is very serious. We may have forgotten it. But God has not. The history of Israel shows the eventual devastating judgement on the accumulated disobedience of God's people. Currently, we are presuming upon the mercy of God – a dangerous presumption. The present House of Bishops has changed in membership considerably since that time and includes many more orthodox bishops.

I call on the House or individual bishops publicly to repudiate those paragraphs in the report *The Nature of Christian Belief* which did the damage. The first is Paragraph 50 which states: 'On the question of whether . . . Christ's tomb that first Easter Day was empty we recognize that scholarship can offer no conclusive demonstration; and the divergent views to be found among scholars of standing are reflected in the thinking of individual bishops'. The second is Paragraph 62 which states: 'The divergences between Christian scholars on the relation of the virginal conception of our Lord to this great mystery [the incarnation], and on the question whether or not that conception is to be regarded as historical fact as well as imagery symbolic of divine truth, have been indicated, and they are reflected in the convictions of members of this House.'

We have noted the 'repentance' entailed in the 2010 clergy signing our Open Letter against multifaith worship. We are still living in the aftermath of that event. But it will not be long before the pluralism and syncretism of our age draws us back into such controversy. So the loosening of our hold on credal doctrine about Jesus should be seen as linked with the marginalization of him inherent in multifaith services. The New Testament strongly condemns those who undermine Christology and the uniqueness of Christ as the only Saviour.

We praise God for the changes for the better and call for a watching brief to be kept so that the Church of England does not permit creeping syncretism in belief or practice.

Homosexuality

It seems very unlikely that the ordination of practising homosexuals will be *officially* accepted under the present Archbishop. But will his successor in a few years' time take a more liberal position?

The real threat lies in the *de facto* acceptance of lay homosexual practice and even of homosexual clergy. A significant number of bishops seem to accept 'committed, faithful' lay homosexual relationships, although some see them only as a lesser evil than promiscuous gay relationships.

Significantly, when Martin Wharton, Bishop of Newcastle, stated publicly in 1997 that 'homosexuality within a loving, permanent relationship is no sin', the Archbishop of York responded by saying: 'I am not persuaded that Bishop Wharton has said or done anything which is contrary to the doctrine, discipline or worship of the Church of England, and which therefore merits my intervention as Archbishop . . .'. The Archbishop assured me that Bishop Wharton, who has not withdrawn his earlier statement, fully accepts the position stated in The House of Bishops' report, *Issues in Human Sexuality.*

It follows that *Issues in Human Sexuality* must be understood as meaning homosexual practice in a loving permanent relationship is not sinful.

Sadly, although the report has not been approved by the General Synod, the fact that many bishops constantly refer to it as their agreed position and affirm solemn allegiance to it, effectively makes it the *de facto* position of the Church (which is, of course, what they want to achieve).

There are only three consolations. First, the report is the official policy of the Church. Second, some 40 per cent of the present House of Bishops were appointed after the report was published and some of them are not happy with it. Third, many individual bishops still believe homosexual practice *is* sinful.

I call upon individual bishops to have the courage to break ranks and state publicly that homosexual practice is sinful in all circumstances, expressing disagreement with the unhelpful aspects of the report and refusing to refer to it as if it has been agreed.

If the Church does not repent of its slide towards permitting homosexual practice, I believe the Lord will judge us by allowing us to have our way, which is an established pattern for his judgement.

One result could be a massive split, worse than that over women's ordination. Whether that would take the form of a huge secession or, if my call to stay within is heeded, lead to the virtual creation of a Church within the Church of England cannot be foreseen.

Another possibility is that, because the position is being changed by bishops *de facto*, rather than through an official synod decision, and also because of the tendency of good people to do nothing in such circumstances, there will not be a point at which a strong reaction takes place. Instead, the Church will eventually wake up to realize the battle is lost.

In the 1997 General Synod debate the House of Bishops effectively ruled out any pro-gay amendments to a fairly innocuous private member's motion commending *Issues in Human Sexuality* for study. Because of this my deep concern is that parishes will relax, feeling the battle is over for the time being. But, for the reasons I've just stated, it isn't. Also experience teaches that the myth spread by the gay lobby that synod approved the report is likely to gain credence. The gay lobby will also do its utmost to influence debate throughout the

Church amid growing political pressure, not least from the European Community which recently approved a mandatory equal opportunities policy covering sexual orientation.

If orthodox parishes say and do nothing their silence will be construed as consent to the serious weaknesses in *Issues in Human Sexuality.*

The only hope is for the parishes to stand up and be counted against this trend now. They could act on the study material I have sent to all the clergy. I call on parishes to wake up and express to their bishops and General Synod representatives their opposition to homosexual practice, and to do it now. I have so designed the resources that to do so is a simple matter. Some parishes are doing this, but will there be enough? If not, I believe God's judgement will be even more severe on our Church than if the battle had been lost through a decision in General Synod.

I call on those in authority to repent of their legitimization of lay homosexual relationships; to require that ordinands are questioned on this issue, and to ensure that no future appointments are made of clergy who are known to be practising homosexuals, whether promiscuous or in a 'committed, faithful relationship'. Early retirement should be offered to those currently in practising homosexual relationships. After all, it is the fault of those who have allowed them in that they are in a position of responsibility within the Church. As long as no progay legislation is passed this will ensure that eventually the Church of England will be cleansed of this serious compromise.

Financial Crisis

Another new factor is the demise of financial endowments from the past. Gone are the days when the dead could keep the church going. Current economies and strategies will not solve the problem. Only repentance leading to spiritual renewal which issues in sacrificial giving so that most churches become, in effect, self-financing will save us from radical cut-backs.

Failing that many churches will simply not survive. Thriving churches cannot keep increasing their quota payments. God is speaking to us through our financial and other crises. But I am not sure we are listening to the urgent whisper of the Spirit.

And Finally . . .

I rejoice in the one, universal body of Christ. I am no denominationalist. But I have to admit that I love the Church of England. It has so much to contribute to the national and universal body of Christ (as well as to receive). But most of the time we, like sheep, keep our heads down 'nibbling' at PCCs and synods, at maintenance and fund raising; at annual reports and five-year plans. We do not stand back to see the whole picture; to gain a sense of long-term perspective; to ask how God sees our lives and ministries and denomination. Like sheep we do not look where we are going. So we are in danger of going astray and facing disaster. The church needs the prophetic ministry to bring perspective, encouragement and to warn people of possible judgement, so that there might be repentance and renewal.

My prayer is that some clergy, including some bishops, will be encouraged to be more prophetic as a result of reading this book. It could be that some readers will be inspired to form prayer groups within local churches or groups of churches, listening to the Lord, praying through current events in the church and society, prompting their church council, writing letters, taking action. This may be applied to members and leaders of any denomination.

One might echo the words of Moses: 'I wish that all the Lord's people were prophets and that the Lord would put his Spirit on them!' But we might not cope with that!

NOTES

Chapter 1

1. Lam. 3.21–22, 32, 40–42; 5.21.
2. Deut. 18.18; Jer. 37.6; 2 Pet. 1.20–21.
3. For examples of the Old Testament prophets' ministry of encouragement, see Judg. 6.8–16; 2 Chron. 15.8; Ezra 6.14. On the other hand they frequently warned of judgement (1 Kings 16.7, cf. v.12; 20.13–14, 36–39; 2 Kings 24.2; Ps. 51.1; Ezek. 6.2; 13.2, 17; 20.46; 21.2; 25.2; 28.1; 29.2; 34.2; 38.2; 39.1; Matt. 13.14). They regularly confronted idolatry (see 1 Kings 14.9; 18.19–22; 2 Kings 1.16; 2 Kings 21.10–15; cf. vv. 1–7; 2 Chron. 15; many passages in Isaiah, Jeremiah, Ezekiel and some in Hosea, Amos, Micah, Habakkuk and Zechariah). In his prophetic messages to the churches of Asia Minor, Jesus also confronted idolatry (see Rev. 2.6, 15) as well as an early form of the Gnostic heresy which, amongst other errors, had a false Christology (see Rev. 2.20–25). They also confronted immorality: Jer. 29.22–23; Lam. 2.14; Ezek. 3.18–21; 22.1–11; 33.26. Jesus' prophetic messages to the churches of Asia Minor include condemnations of sexual immorality (see Rev. 2.6, 14, 20–23). On injustice see, for example, Deut. 27.19; Ps. 33.5; Prov. 20.10, 23; Isa. 10.1–2; 58; Amos 5.21–24; 8.4–7.
4. Dan. 9.2, 24; Acts 3.24; Rev. 1.3; 22.7, 10, 18.
5. Eph. 2.20; 3.5. Commenting on Eph. 2.20, J. Armitage Robinson writes, 'the whole context makes it abundantly clear that Paul is not taking us back from the New Covenant to the Old – not speaking of Old Testament prophets in the past – when he says that the apostles and prophets are the foundation of the new House of God.' (*St Paul's Epistle to the Ephesians*, Macmillan, p. 69). See also my paper 'The Challenge of the Housechurches', in *Latimer Studies 27*, Tony Higton and Gilbert Kirby, Latimer House, Oxford 1988, pp. 20ff.

Chapter 2

1. Matt. 5.22, 29–30; 10.28; 18.8–9; 23.33; 25.41, 46; Mark 9.43, 45, 47; Luke 12.5; 16.23. (This list includes parallels.)
2. A combination of attraction and awe, in this case felt in historic churches or during liturgy and ceremonial.
3. Deut. 18.20; cf. Jer. 14.13–16; Ezek. 28.31.
4. Acts 7.52; cf. 1 Kings 19.14; 2 Chron. 24.19; 36.16; Neh. 9.26, 30; Isa. 30.9–11; Jer. 25.4–7; 32.3; 35.15; Mic. 2.6

Chapter 3

1. e.g. Jeroboam – to his wife (1 Kings 14.10); Baasha (1 Kings 16.1); Ahab (1 Kings 21.10); Pashur (Jer. 20.3ff); Hananiah (Jer. 28.15f); Belshazzar (Dan. 5.23); Herod (Mark 6.18); but also indirectly, e.g. Rezin and Pekah (Isa. 7.8; 8.6; 9.11); Sennacherib (Isa. 37.21ff.); Shallum (Jer. 22.11ff.).
2. Isa. 44.8–20; 45.5–6, 16–22; cf. Deut. 4.39; 32.39; 1 Kings 8.60; Joel 2.27.
3. See *Jesus the Only Saviour*, Tony and Patricia Higton (Monarch, 1993) available with tapes from ABWON, Emmanuel Church, Main Road, Hawkwell, Hockley, Essex SS5 4NR.
4. The conservative, evangelical Anglican pressure group.
5. The Crown Appointments Commission is responsible for recommending to the Prime Minister two names in order of priority as candidates for a particular bishopric. It consists of the archbishops, the Prime Minister's Appointments Secretary, other dignitaries, General Synod representatives and representatives from the diocese in question.
6. *Sexuality and the Church*, Tony Higton (ed.) (ABWON, revised 1987) available from ABWON (address as above). Much of this booklet is still relevant, particularly the chapters on 'Heterosexuality in the Bible' and 'Homosexuality in the Bible' by Dr Gordon Wenham; the historical chapter 'Homosexuality in the Early Church' by Prof. David Wright and the medical chapter.
7. *Jesus the Only Saviour* (ABWON, address as above).

Chapter 4

1. 1 Cor. 14.29; 1 Thess. 5.20–21; 1 John 4.1.
2. Isa. 30.21; Jer. 31.33; Rom. 8.16; Col. 3.

3. See Acts 15, especially vv. 6, 7, 19, 22, 25, 28.
4. Details of the Alpha Course are available from Holy Trinity Church, Brompton Road, London SW7 1JA.
5. These resources may be purchased from ABWON (address as above).
6. Details of Time Ministries International are available from Emmanuel Church, Main Road, Hawkwell, Hockley, Essex SS5 4NR
7. See Ps. 11.7; 33.5; 61.8; Isa. 9.7; 11.4; 16.5; 30.18; 33.5; 42.1, 4.
8. Deut. 27.19; Prov. 20.10, 23; Isa. 10.1–2; Amos 8.4–7.
9. Lev. 19.33–34; Ps. 82.1–4; Isa. 56.1; Jer. 22.3; Mic. 6.8.
10. Lev. 25.35–38; Deut. 24.6, 17, 19–21; 15.3.

Chapter 5

1. Our own Time Ministries strategy and resources which have been adopted in 1000 churches around the world have been used by God to bring churches into a dynamic, outward-looking unity. Details from Time Ministries International (address as above).

Chapter 6

1. See Gal. 1.7–9 where he says those perverting the gospel should be 'eternally condemned'. Similarly Gal. 5.12 where he says he wishes those teaching circumcision as essential to salvation would 'go the whole way and emasculate themselves!'
2. 2 Kings 17.13; Ezek. 3.17–19; Jer. 25.4–5; 35.15; 44.4; Zech. 1.4.
3. 1 Kings 22.8; Isa. 30.10; Jer. 26, 27.14–15; Mic. 2.6.
4. Jer. 6.13–15; Ezek. 13.10–12; Mic. 3.5.
5. *My Reasons for Leaving the Church of England*, Reg Burrows, 20.3.94 (a duplicated leaflet).
6. Para. 148. I would want to add that unfortunately the relevant doctrinal statements are not specified, e.g. Article 8 that there is salvation only in the name of Christ, not in any religious practice. Article 11 that we are only saved through Christ, not works. Article 13 that works done before the grace of Christ and reception of the Holy Spirit are not pleasing to God because they do not spring from faith in Christ.
7. *The Oxford English Dictionary* (2nd edition, 1989) definition of an 'apostate'.

8. The Greek *apostasia* is used in Acts 21.21 where Paul is not being accused by the Jewish believers of totally abandoning the faith, but encouraging those Jews who believe in Christ to abandon such traditonal customs as circumcision. *Apostasia* here does not mean total abandonment, but rather partial abandonment of the faith. It is also used in 2 Thess. 2.3 where the word is used of the final eschatalogical revolt against God. A similar word *apostenai* is used in Heb. 3.12 where the concern of the writer is not of the recipients abandoning the whole of the faith, including belief in God, morality, etc., but reverting to Judaism. So the New Testament use of *aphistemi* and its derivatives does not exclusively refer to total abandonment of the faith, but to matters such as abandoning Jewish ceremonial.
9. 1 Kings 1.22–27, 32–44 Elijah rebuked Ahab (1 Kings 18.18; 21.17–29) and Ahaziah (2 Kings 1.15–17) but he recognized Ahab's repentance which averted God's judgement (1 Kings 21.28–29). Elisha rebuked Joram, the evil king of Israel but on the same occasion showed respect to Jehoshaphat, king of Judah (2 Kings 3.11–15). He also later warned Joram of ambushes set by the Aramaeans (2 Kings 6.8–10; this passage probably refers to Joram). Jehu the seer rebuked Jehoshaphat for co-operating with Ahab, but immediately commended him for his opposition to idolatry and his determination to seek the Lord (2 Chron. 19.1–3). Isaiah rebuked Hezekiah (2 Kings 20.12–19) but he joined in intercession with him in the face of Sennacherib's invasion (2 Chron. 32.20). Jeremiah prophesied judgement on Zedekiah (Jer. 21.3–22.30) but gave him great reassurance in the face of the Babylonian invasion (Jer. 38.14–27).
10. *Christian Herald*, Opinion column, 28.1.95.
11. Gen. 19.16; 2 Sam. 24.1–14; Neh. 9.16–31; 13.15–22; Ps. 51.1; Isa. 55.7; Dan. 9.9, 18; Hab. 3.2; Zech. 1.12–16; Rom. 11.30–31; 1 Tim. 1.13; Jas. 2.13.
12. Rev. 2.21; cf. 2.5, 16; 3.3, 19–20.
13. Rev. 2.7, 17, 26–29; 3.5–6, 21–22.

Chapter 7

1. Rom. 16.17–18; cf. 2 Thess. 3.6, 14; Titus 3.10.
2. 2 John 10; cf. Gal. 1.8–9 where Paul says teachers undermining

the gospel (the context is of Judaizers) should be eternally condemned. Some Christians quote 2 Cor. 6.14–18 as relevant, but it actually refers to separation from unbelievers, not fellow Christians. The same is true of 2 Tim. 3.1–5, but v. 5 seems to refer to nominal Christians.

3. Matt. 18.15–17; cf. 1 Cor. 5; Titus 3.10–11; Jas. 5.19–20.
4. John 10.16; Acts 4.32; Rom 15.5; Gal 3.28; Eph. 4.13; Col. 2.2.
5. Article in *Crossway* magazine, autumn 1996, by Bishop Barry Shucksmith of the Free Church of England.
6. *Mainstream* magazine, summer 1996, published by Banner Ministries, p. 1.
7. *Mainstream*, pp 1–2.
8. See Ps 119.11, 52, 105; John 8.51; Rom. 15.4; Heb 4.12.
9. Ps. 119.14, 16, 77, 97, 159, 167, 172.
10. Neh 9.16–17, 26–27, 31.
11. *Distinctive Ideas of the Old Testament*, Epworth, London, 1962, pp. 99f.
12. *Distinctive Ideas*, p. 102.
13. *Distinctive Ideas*, pp. 120f.
14. Mal 1.6–14; 2.1–16; 3.5–15.
15. See Acts 6, 12, 15; Rom 14–16; 1 Cor. 1.3; 3; 5; 11; 2 Cor. 12; Gal. 2; 4; Phil. 4; 1 Thess. 4; 2 Thess. 3; 1 Tim. 6; Titus; Jas. 4; 1 John; 3 John; Jude; Rev. 2.
16. Articles 2, 4, 11, 13 and 18.
17. General Synod Constitution, Article 7.
18. In a talk at an Anglican Renewal Ministries conference.

Chapter 8

1. *Canterbury Tales*, Channel 4, 1996.